LETTERS TO JOSEPH PRIESTLEY

TAKEN FROM MY LIBRARY SHELF
AND REPRINTED IN LIKE FORM
Original Fonts Version
Don Milton

All Text, Images, and Text Images
Copyright 2009 Don Milton
All Rights Reserved

Letters to Joseph Priestley

ABOUT THE EDITOR/PUBLISHER

Don Milton writes, edits, and publishes books on Courtship and Christian Marriage as well as Law & Justice. He is the author of Prince of Sumba, Husband to Many Wives and is currently working on a historical novel.

ABOUT MARTIN MADAN

In 1746, forty one years before the Reverend Martin Madan wrote this book, he founded the London Lock Hospital. London Lock was the first voluntary hospital that treated venereal disease.[1] Shortly after Madan founded the Lock Hospital, the institution opened a new building and it became known as *The Female Hospital*. He then began to hold worship services in areas of the hospital *that afforded him the ability to preach as well as to lead a congregation in the singing of hymns* but soon it became crowded, so he set out to build a chapel. With donations from wealthy patrons he was able to build a chapel that seated up to eight hundred people.[2] This may not seem large compared with today's mega-churches but it's still a very large fellowship and it was one of the largest of his day. The wonderful thing about Madan's chapel was that it received enough in tithes to become a strong source of support for the hospital.[3] It was there that the singing of hymns first took hold as part of Christian worship.[4] The members of Lock Chapel sang from a hymnal that Madan, himself, had published. He published the hymnal as a benefit to future generations as well as to raise money for the hospital.[5] From the Chapel at the Lock, hymn singing spread quickly throughout the English speaking world with Madan's hymnal the standard. His mastery of musical worship brought thousands to the Chapel at the Lock and his hymns have brought many more thousands to a saving

About the Author - Martin Madan

knowledge of our Lord.6 In less than thirty short years from the first printing of Madan's hymnal, fully two thirds of the hymns sung, even in the parishes of the Church of England, had been lifted; *word for word, note for note, from Madan's own hymnal*. Madan's hymnal had in fact become the core of the Church of England's hymnal.7 The Baptists' hymnal came out twenty five years after Madan's.8 The hymnal that he published was called A Collection of Psalm and Hymn Tunes Never Published Before, the proceeds from which were for the benefit of the Lock Hospital.

Madan held the position of Chaplain at the Lock till the day he died. This was partly due to the fact that he eclipsed all of his contemporaries in promoting, as well as defending, the faith. It was Madan who defended Whitefield and the Methodists against the vicious satire of playwright, Samuel Foote, in 1760, (See his Exhortatory Address to the Brethren in the Faith of Christ reissued by Don Milton) so it was not surprising that he continued to defend the faith and biblical morality till the day he went to be with the Lord."9

Madan's translation of Juvenal and Persius from Latin to English, which he published in 1789, two years after this book, contained copious explanatory notes. Today it remains unmatched in thoroughness.10 On occasion he still preached at the Lock Chapel and he wrote dozens of letters excoriating those who would gamble on the horse races.11

Two years before the publication of this book, In 1785, he excoriated another group of rascals, the judges of England, for their inconsistency in rendering justice. In his seminal work, Executive Justice, he outlined the need for sure and swift punishment of criminals. After his death he was falsely accused of having favored hanging for theft, but he stated in the very book that they quoted out of context against him, that he agreed with the maxim that '*a less punishment, which is certain, will do more good than a greater [punishment], which is uncertain.*'[12] Despite all these accomplishments, not to mention his many published sermons, Christian historians have failed to chronicle his ministry in their accounts of the great evangelists of the Eighteenth Century, not to mention the great legal minds of the Eighteenth Century. This and other books in this series, will attempt to correct that deficiency, a deficiency which has left an important part of Church history unrecorded; the transition from singing Psalms to singing hymns. And it was that transition that the Lord used to spark the great revivals of the hundred years that followed Madan's ministry. Prior to Martin Madan's successful promotion of hymn singing, there were only random cases of hymn singing. A church here, or a church there would allow hymn singing, and Christians at non-church venues as well as at dissenting churches sang hymns. However, it took the success of the Reverend Martin Madan's chapel and its music to make it acceptable. The new hymn singing combined biblical concepts with calls to repentance into a moving form of worship. The hymn provides a way for biblical concepts to be presented in poetry set to music. Many lost souls have been deaf to all other forms of preaching, but have been converted by the hearing of a single hymn.

As you read this book, may you be blessed in knowing that its author was the man who polished some of the most famous words in today's hymnals, the man who composed and arranged the music behind many of those hymns, and the man who cared for and counseled the cast aside women of his time; Martin Madan, the Father of the Evangelical Hymnal.

The preceding *About Martin Madan* section as well as the following footnotes are used with permission, having been gleaned from Prince of Sumba, Husband to Many Wives, Chapter 12 - Martin Madan, A Memory of Love by Don Milton - Copyright 2009

1. "The first special hospital was the Lock Hospital near Hyde Park Corner, founded in 1746 by Martin Madan, who became its first chaplain."
A History of English Philanthropy
by Benjamin Kirkman Gray
London - P.S. King & Son, Orchard House, Westminster - 1905

The following is an account of some of the types of patients that could be found at the Lock Hospital.

"There are merit-mongers, among the most abandoned sinners. Two women were, some time since, admitted into the Lock Hospital, in order to be cured of a very criminal disease. Mr. Madan, who visited them during their confinement, laboured to convince them of their sin and spiritual danger, 'Truly,' said one of them, 'I am by no means so bad as some of my profession are : for I never picked any man's pocket, in my life.' The other said, 'I cannot affirm that I never picked a man's pocket; but I have this in my favour, that I never admitted any man in my company, on a Sunday, until after nine at night.'
The Works of Augustus M. Toplady page 168.

About the Author - Martin Madan

You will remember Toplady as the writer of that famous hymn, Rock of Ages. He was a very close friend and admirer of the Reverend Martin Madan, having also preached at the Lock Chapel.

Good News from Heaven; or, the Gospel a Joyful Sound. At the Lock Chapel, near Hyde Park Corner, June 19, 1774. By the Reverend Augustus Toplady.

Recorded on page 375 of The Monthly Review Volume 52 1775

Madan wrote a tract concerning the sequence of events that led to the conversion of one such prostitute. Despite her conversion and new way of living, she soon died of the illnesses she acquired as a prostitute. This is chronicled in: *A Remarkable and surprising account of the abandoned life, happy conversion, and comfortable death of Fanny Sidney, a young gentlewoman, who died in London in April, 1763, aged 26 years.* By the Reverend Martin Madan

2. "The Lock Chapel was (officially) opened March 28, 1762" but the Reverend Martin Madan conducted services prior to that in other areas of the institution that afforded him the ability to preach as well as to lead the congregation in the singing of hymns.

Dictionary of National Biography - Edited by Sidney Lee - McMillan and Co.1893 - Page 288

Through Martin's exertions a new chapel, capable of seating 800 persons, was erected in the garden of the hospital, he himself contributing 100 pounds.[100 pounds converts to $20,000 in today's U.S. dollars. University of Michigan conversion table.] It was opened on March 28, 1762 and by 1765 was entirely free of debt.

The Madan Family and Maddens in Ireland and

About the Author - Martin Madan

England By Falconer Madan 1933 - Page 112

3. "In the case of the Lock Hospital, the musical movement coincided with the Evangelical. Its chapel was used not only by its inmates, but by a strongly contrasting *West End Evangelical congregation who rented sittings.*"

These rented pews helped pay for the expenses of the hospital.

The Princeton Theological Review - Volume XII - 1914

The Princeton University Press - Princeton, N.J. - Page 87

4. "He (William Romaine) held the extreme Calvinistic position as to the exclusive use of inspired words in Praise, and was able to impose his views upon his own congregation. But he could not stay the rising tide of Hymn singing or make a breach between the Gospel and the Hymns of the Revival. *In Martin Madan the new Hymn singing found an effective sponsor.* The humorous and sturdy John Berridge was as early on the field as Madan, but less effective."

The Princeton Theological Review - Volume XII - 1914

The Princeton University Press - Princeton, N.J. - Page 73,74

5. In the preface to the Hymnal that the Reverend Martin Madan published, "The Collection of Psalm and Hymn Tunes sung at the Chapel of the Lock Hospital" Mr. Madan writes:

"I have at last, with no small care and trouble, completed this Book of Tunes for the use of the Chapel; and as the publication of them may be of service to the Charity, I must desire your acceptance of

About the Author - Martin Madan

the Entire Copy, hoping that, by the sale of this Music, some addition may be made to your fund for maintaining and promoting the charitable work which you have undertaken."

6. The Church of England's hymnal began with Martin Madan's Collection of Psalms and Hymns (1760).

The New Schaff-Herzog Encyclopedia of Religious Knowledge by Johann Jakob Herzog, Philip Schaff, and others. Copyright 1909

7. In 1788, the publisher of the fifth edition of the Church of England hymnal, "appropriated fully two thirds of the contents of Madan's Collection."

The Princeton Theological Review - Volume XII - 1914

The Princeton University Press - Princeton, N.J. - Page 76

8. The first Baptist hymn-book was Rippon's (1787).

The New Schaff-Herzog Encyclopedia of Religious Knowledge by Johann Jakob Herzog, Philip Schaff, and others. Copyright 1909

9. It was Martin Madan who defended Whitefield and the Methodists against the vicious satire of playwright, Samuel Foote in his Exhortatory address to the brethren in the faith of Christ published in 1760

10. A New and Literal Translation of Juvenal and Persius; with Copious Explanatory Notes, by which these difficult satirists are rendered easy and familiar to the reader. In Two Volumes.

By the Rev. M. Madan -Printed for the Editor, at Mr. Lewis's, No 157, Swallow-Street, Near Piccadilly MDCCLXXXIX (1789)

11. "It was formerly the abode of the celebrated [famous] Dr. Madan [Martin Madan], of whom we

About the Author - Martin Madan

have given an account. During his residence here, [Birmingham, England] he interposed his authority as a magistrate, to prevent the introduction of illegal games into the town during the race week; he gave notice to those persons, who were in the habit of letting [renting] their houses for this purpose, that it was contrary to the laws of their country, and if they persisted in doing it, they must take consequences. Several tradespeople, who disregarded this notice, were sent to prison, which so exasperated the inhabitants, that they burnt his effigy, near the spot where the pump now stands."

Some Particulars Relating to the History of Epsom by Henry Pownall 1825

"I possess twenty-three letters from him to George Hardinge, Esq., M.P., July 9, 1789-March 14, 1790, [Against illegal gaming] written in good spirits and with some wit."

The Madan Family by Falconer Madan 1933

"Mr. Madan, however, the most respectable clergyman in the town, [Birmingham] preaching [1787-1789] and publishing... [against Priestley's Unitarianism] ...I addressed a number of "Familiar Letters to the Inhabitants of Birmingham," in our defence."

An Appeal to the Serious and Candid Professors of Christianity By Joseph Priestley - Page 105

12. Thoughts on Executive Justice with respect to our Criminal Laws Published in 1785 - Page 63

ERRATA.

P. 57. l. 6. *r.* ȣx αρπαγμον.
P. 74. l. 2. *r.* αμεμπ]ος.
P. 86. l. 12. *r.* משיחים.
P. 87. l. 9. *r.* משיח.
P. 110. l. 12. *r.* act.
P. 128. l. 4. *dele* the first in.

LETTERS

TO

JOSEPH PRIESTLEY, LL.D. F.R.S.

LETTERS

TO

JOSEPH PRIESTLEY, LL.D. F.R.S.

OCCASIONED BY

HIS LATE CONTROVERSIAL WRITINGS.

BY THE REV. M. MADAN.

HE THAT BELIEVETH NOT GOD, HATH MADE HIM A LIAR, BECAUSE HE BELIEVETH NOT THE RECORD THAT GOD GAVE OF HIS SON.
1 *John* v. 10.

Be that my task, replies a gloomy clerk,
Sworn foe to myst'ry, yet divinely dark:
Whose pious hope aspires to see the day
When moral evidence shall quite decay:
And damns implicit faith and holy lies,
Prompt to impose, and fond to dogmatize.
DUNCIAD IV.

LONDON:
PRINTED FOR J. DODSLEY, PALL-MALL.

M.DCC.LXXXVII.

ADVERTISEMENT.

THE *Letters* quoted in the following papers are, Dr. P.'s *letters* to Dr. *Horne*—to the *Young Men*, &c.—to Dr. *Price*—and to the Rev. Mr. *Parkhurst*; all lately published together in one pamphlet.

LETTERS

TO

D<small>R</small>. PRIESTLY,

OCCASIONED BY

HIS LATE PUBLICATIONS.

LETTER I.

May 1787

S I R,

I HAVE not the honour of the least perſonal acquaintance with you, but as you profeſs yourſelf to write from " a ſincere *love of* " *truth*," I will not aim at any apology for troubling you with a few letters, on ſome of the ſubjects which

which you have so largely, and so freely treated in your publications. As the very reverse of all your propositions contains the *only* hope of salvation which I can entertain, either for myself or others, you must allow my views of the matter to be too important to admit of any ceremony between us.

As to entering into controversy about *fathers* and *ecclesiastical histories*, I certainly shall not, there is no end of such disputations; nor do I know any real use of them, where the matter in debate cannot be ascertained, but on the testimony, the single testimony, of *Divine Revelation*. Here, Sir, I shall fix my foot, as on the great rock of everlasting truth, and from hence direct my every argument against your writings.

Therefore, with my *Hebrew* Bible before me, as the great foundation of all the religious truth which we are acquainted with, together with the *New Testament*, as the best, and indeed the only infallible comment on the *Hebrew* S. S. I will venture an attack on the confident and monstrous assertions of *Dr. Priestly*.

I do not enter upon this, as calling in question the learning and ability of others your opponents; I highly honour them, and prefer them far beyond any that I can pretend to: but when doctrines sub-

subversive of *Christianity itself*, are not only published under a notion of *Christian truth* — when these are recommended to the notice and attention of the youth in our two great seminaries of learning, so that the rising generation may come forth, like the *Ægyptian* swarms, to corrupt the land—it is high time for every man that calls himself a *Christian*, who has a head to think, and an hand to write, to bear an open and unreserved testimony on the occasion. My excuse, therefore, for presuming to follow those, who are so much abler than myself, must be contained in *David*'s answer to *Eliab* — " Is " THERE NOT A CAUSE ?"

The

The first great point in true religion, is, to be acquainted with the true object of worship; for, without *this*, there can be no true worship; and indeed from the knowledge of this all other truths must flow, as from their fountain-head—if this be corrupt, so must they. Dr. P. the great champion of the modern *Unitarians*, with his allies, the apostate*, judicially-blinded Jews, and the deceived *Mahometans* †, leads up all his forces to secure this point; well knowing that all he says about the *person of Christ* must utterly be lost, and fall into the enemies hands, unless

* If. vi. 9, 10, with Acts xxviii. 25—7.
† Letter to Parkhurst, 185.

a God, subsisting in *one person only*, be established, as the only *Lord God*, maker of heaven and earth. Hence his treatment of the doctrine of the *Trinity*, comparing it to that of *transubstantiation* in point of absurdity, both with respect to itself, and to the arguments which are brought to support it; concealing from his readers one essential argument against the *latter*, I mean that of our outward senses, such as our seeing, feeling, taste, and smelling, none of which are in the least concerned with regard to the *former*.

This, Sir, must be allowed a matter of pure revelation; and as I verily believe that God could not
require

require his people to worship him for 4,000 years together, without revealing himself to them as the true object of worship; so I do as verily believe, that the *name*, or *names*, by which he proposed himself to their knowledge and worship, are faithfully recorded by *Moses*, as well as by all the other writers of the *Hebrew* S. S.

The first name which we meet with, stands the third word in the Old Testament, namely אלהים, ALEIM.— This word is *plural* in *sense* as well as in *form*, and all that Dr. P. and his allies can say, can no more make it singular, than they can make its singular, אלה, plural. The singular word God, which Dr. P. has given his readers, as standing in Gen. i. in our *English* tranſlation, anſwering his purpoſe much better, he would rather have them think that *Moſes* wrote in *Engliſh*, than in a language which opens the earlieſt account of the Deity, with giving him a *plural* name. I know full well how ill this name ſuits with the *Unitarian* ſcheme, as likewiſe with the *Arian*, and certain others, and therefore am not in the leaſt ſurpriſed, that *Unitarians*, *Arians*, &c. ſhould endeavour (however vainly) to evade the force of it;—but there it ſtands, and there it will ſtand, as a direct and poſitive teſtimony to a *plurality* in the Deity;

Deity; and the *gates of hell shall not prevail against it.*

As I mean brevity in this, and all my other letters, I will not enter into the idle cavils, or, in other words, into *the perverse disputings of men* * *of corrupt minds, who are destitute of the truth;* but, having stated the above as an undeniable *matter of fact,* on the testimony of the *Hebrew* Bible, only refer you to the learned Mr. PARKHURST's *Heb.* and *Eng.* Lexicon, for a farther explanation of the matter, under אלה, N° II.; and, taking my leave for the present, subscribe myself,

SIR,

Your humble servant.

* 1 Tim. vi. 5.

LETTER II.

SIR,

SINCE I wrote my laſt, I have been thinking to what little purpoſe I recommended the word אלהים to your obſervation on the authority of the *Hebrew* S. S. for, on looking into your letter to Mr. *Parkhurſt*, I find the following paragraph :—

"Admitting the plural form of
"the word ſignifying *God* to be
"a juſt foundation for believing
"that there is a plurality in the
"divine eſſence, it is only in one
"particular language, which can
"no

" no more be proved to be of di-
" vine origin than any other lan-
" guage, and may not even have
" been the moſt ancient; ſo that
" it might be merely accidental,
" that this word, as well as ſeveral
" others in the ſame language, and
" many in all languages, had a plu-
" ral, and not a ſingular form."

The ſeveral members of which this moſt ſingular paragraph is compoſed, may, I think, be looked upon as furniſhing ample matter for another letter.

In a paragraph preceding, you ſpeak of the futility of the argument, which is grounded on the plural word *Aleim*, to prove a plurality in the divine eſſence; and
tell

tell us, that " *Basnage* and others " have shewn the futility of it." The futility of what, Sir? Do you mean that *Basnage* and others have shewn a futility in construing a *plural* word to have a *plural* meaning? or, that it is futile to lay any stress on a plural word, as proving that the subject to which it is applied has, in some respect or other, a *plurality* in it? I am very certain that neither *Basnage*, Dr. P. or any other, can shew this, because it cannot be shewn, if, by *shewn*, you mean proved, or demonstrated; it involves all rules of construction in such darkness and uncertainty, as to destroy the chief use of all language whatsoever,

ever, which is, to communicate with its best precision and certainty those ideas of which it treats.

"Admitting," say you, "the "plural *form* of the word signify- "ing God"—Here, Sir, you are for admitting, what must be denied, *i.e.* that the word *Aleim* signifies God, I mean in its *radical*, true *grammatical* sense—it is indeed *translated* God, as by that word we understand the Supreme Being; and, perhaps, therefore the best word which our language could afford. But, in the first place, the word God is *singular*, *Aleim* is *plural*; in the next place, God is an arbitrary word, only by custom and use adapted to express
the

the common idea which we annex to it: whereas אלהים, from אלה to *curse* or *denounce a curse*, implies, as a *noun* in the *plural*, persons *denouncing a curse*; so persons *under an oath*, or *sworn* to the *performance of something*.—It is a characteristic of the *Hebrew*, which proves it not of *human* origin, that every word is derived from some fixed root, which root has a meaning expressive of the nature, quality, or circumstances of the thing, or action, expressed by the word.—Hence, *Aleim* cannot be adequately expressed by any single arbitrary word in any other language. Translators must do as well as they can, by substituting the

the best word which the language into which they translate affords, however in itself inadequate to the precise and full meaning of the original, for the same reason that artists must work with the tools they have—they cannot be expected to use such as they have not.—Hence *God* and *Lord* are substituted for אלהים and יהוה; so in Greek Θεος and Κυριος, none of which adequately express the *Hebrew*. Now, Sir, you assert, "that we are no "where taught in the Old Testa- "ment, that this mysterious doc- "trine of *three divine denouncers of* "*a conditional curse* (at the idea "of which the mind recoils)" say you (and very consistently with
your

your scheme) " is to be inferred " from" the *form* of the word " *Aleim*."—Letters, p. 151.

Do you not here evade the question? No more is to be inferred from the mere *form* of the word, than that it is *plural*.—The true question is concerning its *radical sense* and *meaning*; which you do not at all enter into.

But " your mind recoils at the " idea." Does it recoil more at this, than at the doctrine of the *Trinity*, the *divinity* of CHRIST, the *atonement*, &c.? Not one jot, if your own writings are an exact copy of your sentiments.

However, it shall be my endeavour to ease your mind, as far as
Scripture

Scripture may do it, with respect to all these points.—And first, as to persons *denouncing a curse*, or *swearing*, signified by the word *Aleim*, I would desire you to consider the following texts in your *Hebrew Bible*, Gen. xxii. 16—18.—Here we find JEHOVAH, the ESSENCE EXISTING, *swearing by* HIMSELF, binding himself by *oath*, to confer certain blessings on *Abraham* and his seed. But, passing over many similar passages, let us come at once to the point of the oath concerning the covenant, by which the *Messiah* was to be made the *High Priest* of his people; I allude Pf. cx. 4. Comp. Heb. vii. 21—28. Now saith the *Apostle*,

C Heb.

Heb. vi. 16, *Men verily swear by the greater, and an oath for confirmation is to them an end of all strife; wherein God, willing more abundantly to shew to the heirs of promise the immutability of his counsel, confirmed it with an oath: That by two immutable things (i.e.* his counsel and his oath) *in which it was impossible for God to lie, we might have a strong consolation, who have fled for refuge to lay hold upon the hope set before us: which hope we have as an anchor of the soul, &c.*

Now, Sir, though doubtless you will say that there is no such thing as the *soul*, yet, surely, this passage fully justifies us in supposing, that there is some idea of an *oath*

in

in the meaning of the word *Aleim*; and that therefore we reasonably conclude, that it expresses not only a *plurality* in the *divine essence*, but holds forth to us some solemn engagement to be performed by the persons in JEHOVAH, or the ESSENCE EXISTING *, in the fulness of time, ratified by *oath*.

Here, lest I should make this letter too long, I will only add that I am,

S I R,

Your humble servant.

* This appears the most literal rendering of יהוה—the great OΩN—Και O HN—Και O ΕΡΧΟΜΕΝΟΣ.—See *Rev.* i. 8.

LETTER III.

SIR,

I NOW proceed in the examination of the rest of your paragraph, transcribed at the beginning of my last.

In order to get rid of the evidence of the plural word *Aleim*, as denoting a plurality in *Jehovah*, you observe, that " it is only in " one particular language;"—and what then? Is not that one particular language* the language in which the NAME of GOD is revealed to us?—Consider diligently, *Ex.* iii. 15.

---

* See Parkh. Pref. to Heb. and Eng. Lexicon, p. ii.

" Which

"Which can no more be prov-
"ed to be of divine origin than
"any other language."—This affertion is equally bold and false: for saying this, I refer you to Exodus xxxi. 18. *And he* (JEHOVAH) *gave unto* MOSES, *when he had made an end* of communing with him upon *Mount Sinai*, two *tables of testimony, tables of stone*, WRITTEN WITH THE FINGER OF ALEIM. Comp. *Deut.* ix. 10, and Exod. xxxii. 16, and then determine, if you can, that the language in which the contents of these tables were written was not the same in which they are now delivered to us, and that "it
"can no more be proved to be of
"divine origin than any other
"language;" though this was

written,

written, and spoken to the people by GOD HIMSELF.—" So that it might be merely accidental that this word had a plural form."—Rotten premises usually produce a rotten conclusion. I do not suppose, at least I am not willing to suppose, that there is a man in the kingdom, learned or unlearned, believer or infidel, except Dr. P. who could have advanced such a proposition as this, that a word evidently plural, and which has as evidently its singular, a word used above two thousand times in the Scriptures, should have assumed a plural form by *mere accident!*—that God himself should both *speak* and *write* it;—that *Moses*, and the sacred *historians*

historians and *prophets*, should use it perpetually in a plural form, and this without any particular intention, but induced thereto by a *merely accidental* form of the word—is much more easily conceived by Dr. P. than by any who do not wish to silence the evidence which it affords for a plurality in JEHOVAH.

I should not, after this, be much surprized, if, for the edification of the youth at our universities, you were to publish a learned treatise, to shew that the first *Hebrew Bible* was collected at the composing-engine of *Laputa*, and thus account for the *accident*; this would furnish you with a more rational con-

conclusion, than that which you have given us.

See, Sir, to what abſurd and wretched ſhifts you are driven, in your oppoſition to the word of God. It ſhall mean *any thing* to favour your ſentiments, it ſhall mean *nothing* to contradict them; and, in order to effect this, you ſcruple not, like another *Alexander*, to cut the knot which you cannot untie.

I now have a word to ſay to you, on ſome ſubjects which are nearly connected with the foregoing; namely, the *divinity* and *preexiſtence* of Jesus Christ; theſe are ſo inſeparable, that the proof of the *former* muſt demonſtrate the *latter*. My

My creed I profess to be, that He is one of the ALEIM, which constitute the *plurality* in the *divine essence*, coequal and coeternal with the other TWO; for that the *plurality* is limited to THREE, all Scripture demonstrates; and I am assured, by authority which I deem *infallible*, that *all Scripture is given by inspiration of God, and that holy men of old spake as they were moved by the* HOLY GHOST, the other divine person in JEHOVAH ALEIM.

Your creed, if you can be said to have any, appears to be like that of the *fool* (Pf. xiv. 1.) *who said in his heart* לא אלהים, there are no *Aleim*. Comp. Pf. liii. 1. If we look into *Deut.* iv. 33, we
are

are told, that JEHOVAH HE IS A-
LEIM, *and there is none elfe befides
him.* Therefore, if we reject him,
we become *Atheifts* in fact, though
Theifts in fpeculation—the argument is very conclufive, and the
fetting up a God *in one perfon*,
whether it be made of filver, or
gold, or wood, or ftone, graven by
art or man's device, or fits en-
fhrined, and furrounded with *fixed
air*, in the brain of a philofopher,
ftill it is an idol, and we know
(fays the great apoftle of the Gentiles) that an *idol is nothing in the
world, and that there is none other
God but one*, 1 Cor. viii. 4; meaning, no doubt, the GOD revealed
in the Hebrew Scriptures to his

people

people of old—*that they might fear that glorious and fearful name* JEHOVAH, *their* ALEIM. *Deut.* xxviii. 58.

With regard to the *person of* CHRIST, you hold him out as not existing before he was born of a woman; " as a mere man like " ourselves, the son of *Joseph* and " *Mary*, capable of misapplying the " Scriptures of the Old Testament, " naturally fallible, peccable, " weak;" in short, just like " other " men."—This, Sir, is carrying *Socinianism* to a greater length than any of your predecessors have done, and is a sad proof of the truth of 2 Tim. iii. 13, *that evil men and seducers shall wax worse and worse, deceiving and being deceived.* However

ever your allies, the modern *Jews*, may hold with you, I am confident that the real followers of *Socinus* would defert you; and as for the *Mahommedans*, from what I recollect of the *Alcoran*, which I once red over in *Sale*'s tranflation, I am almoft as confident, that if you were to go, and to have your writings publifhed at *Conftantinople*, you would run the hazard of being impaled for thus reviling " *Jefus* the Son of *Mary*," " the *Word of*, and *from*, GOD."

The length of this letter admonifhes me to put off any further obfervations, till a future opportunity.

I am, SIR,
Yours, &c.

LET-

LETTER IV.

WHO is this that cometh from Edom, with dyed garments from Bozrah? this that is glorious in his apparel, travelling in the greatness of his strength? I that speak in righteousness, mighty to save.

Wherefore art thou red in thine apparel, and thy garments like him that treadeth in the wine-fat?

I have trodden the wine-press alone, and of the people there was none with me: for I will tread them in mine anger, and trample them in my fury; and their blood shall be sprinkled on my garments, and I will stain all

all my raiment. For the day of vengeance is in mine heart, and the year of my redeemed is come.

And I looked, and there was none to help; and I wondered that there was none to uphold: therefore mine own arm brought salvation to me, and my fury it upheld me. If. lxiii. 1—5.

"Of whom speaketh the pro-
"phet this? of himself, or of some
"other man?"—An inspired apostle, and therefore an infallible interpreter, tells us, that *the testimony of* JESUS *is the spirit of prophecy;* doubtless of *this prophecy:*—for, says he, *He was clothed with a vesture dipped in blood, and his name is called* THE WORD OF GOD. See Rev. xix. 13.—*And again,* ver. 15, 16,
He

He treadeth the wine-press of the fierceness and wrath of Almighty God. And he hath on his vesture and on his thigh a name written, KING OF KINGS *and* LORD OF LORDS.

Now, Sir, think on these things, compare these most transcendently magnificent descriptions of the Redeemer, with your " fallible, " peccable, weak, ignorant, mere " man;" and, if you are not *past feeling*, one should think that you can do nothing less than collect your works together, amounting to the enormous sum of *fifteen pounds ten shillings* for a copy of the whole, and commit them to the flames. You have a strong precedent

cedent for this, Acts xix. 19, where *many of them who used curious arts, brought their books together, and burned them before all men: and they counted the price of them, and found it fifty thousand pieces of silver*, about £.1,500 of our money. This was in consequence of *the name of the* Lord Jesus *being magnified*, ver. 17; and why may not the same cause produce the same effects in *Dr. P.* with respect to his books, as it did in these *Ephesian* magicians with respect to theirs? I do not mean, Sir, by this, to charge you with being a *conjurer*—I am far from any such thought.

The incarnation of one of the
Aleim

Aleim in Jehovah, or of one of the persons in the divine essence, is an idea which did not owe its original to the days of the *New Testament*; it pervades the whole of the law and of the prophets.—*The seed of the woman,* promised Gen. iii. 15. was the foundation of it; and this is explained in the subsequent parts of the *Hebrew Scriptures* at *divers times,* and *in divers manners.* Sometimes, even by matters of fact, in which the very thing itself was exhibited. For instance, *Josh.* v. 13, &c.

It came to pass, that when Joshua *was by* Jericho, *that he lift up his eyes and looked, and behold, there stood* A MAN *over against him, with*
his

his sword drawn in his hand; and Joshua *went unto him, and said unto him, Art thou for us, or for our adversaries?*

And he (THE MAN) *said, Nay; but as Prince of the host of* Jehovah *am I now come. And* Joshua *fell with his face to the earth, and did worship, and said unto him, What saith my Lord*—אדני *unto his servant?*

And the Prince of the host of Jehovah *said unto* Joshua, *Loose thy shoe from off thy foot, for the place whereon thou standest is holy.* (Comp. Exod. iii. 5.)

(*Now* Jericho *was straitly shut up because of the children of* Israel; *none went out and none came in.*)

And

And Jehovah *said*, &c.—This MAN is here evidently called JEHOVAH.—Again; the same person appeared to *Manoah* and his wife; *Judges* xiii. 3; where he is called מלאך יהוה the *Angel, Messenger,* or *Sent one*, of *Jehovah*. When *Manoah* asked the name of this איש האלהים *Man of God*, as they called him, supposing him a *prophet* (Comp. Deut. xxxiii. 1), this august personage replies, *Why askest thou thus after my name, seeing it is* פלאי *Wonderful*, ver. 18. Now let us compare this with *Is.* ix. 6. and we shall find, that this very name פלא *Wonderful*, is one of the titles of the *Messiah*, with the ad-

dition

dition of * *Counsellor—the Mighty God—the Everlasting Father—the Prince of Peace.*

I will trouble you but with one more instance, to prove the appearance of a person in *Jehovah*, under the *Old Testament*, in the form of A MAN, in token of his future incarnation—and that stands recorded Gen. xxxii. 24. *And* Jacob *was left alone, and there wrestled* A MAN *with him,* &c.— *And Jacob asked him, and said,* (ver. 29) *Tell me, I pray thee, thy name: and he said, Wherefore is it that thou dost ask after my name? and he blessed him there. And* Jacob *called the name of the place* Peniel; *for I*

---

* Zech. vi. 13.

have

have seen God האלהים: *face to face, and my life is preserved.*

If, after reading and attentively considering this passage, we can doubt who this person was, who wrestled with *Jacob*, under an *human form*, let the prophet *Hosea* be called in to clear up the matter, (chap. xii. 3—5.) *He* (i. e. *Jacob*) *took his brother by the heel in the womb, and by his strength he had power with God: yea, he had power over the* ANGEL, *and prevailed: he wept, and made supplication unto Him: He found him in* BETHEL, *there He spake with us—even* ויהוה אלהי JEHOVAH ALEIM OF HOSTS, צבאות יהוה זכרו JEHOVAH IS HIS MEMORIAL.

See also the appearance of the מלאך יהוה the *Angel Jehovah*, to *Gideon*, Judges, vi. 11—24. and his receiving divine honour and worship, ver. 18—24.

I release myself, and you, from proceeding any further at present; and am,

SIR, &c.

LETTER V.

SIR,

YOU may observe that I have kept my word, and that I have said nothing from primitive Christians, councils, ancient fathers, or church histories—I chuse to let the Scriptures speak for themselves; for, if we believe not *Moses and the prophets, neither shall we believe though one rose from the dead.* Had I an inclination to puzzle the cause, I would go to human authorities: but what men say, or have said—what they think, or have thought—ought to be of no concern with us, on subjects like these,

these, where the word of God can alone decide: therein is contained the mind of God, and to that we must go for information, if we really desire to know it. Here there are no vain disputations, no subtle and perplexing reasonings, no jargon of scholastic terms, no differences, no contradictions—the sacred penmen were all actuated by one spirit; they all spake the same thing, aimed at the same point, and — THUS SAITH THE LORD—their simple argument for our believing what they said;—and I verily believe, that neither yourself, your friend *Dr. Price*, or any other, however learned he may be, can produce so good a one.

I there-

I therefore would venture to advise you, Sir, not only to burn your own books (as mentioned in my fourth letter) but every other that would draw you from *this*. Our *Saviour* recommended the above simple argument to the Jews of his day, who seem to me to have thought of him pretty much as you do.—*Search the scriptures*, says he, *they are they which testify of me*, *John*, v. 39; and again, ver. 46. *Had ye believed Moses, ye would have believed me: for he wrote of me— But if ye believe not his writings, how should you believe my words?* Now, Sir, do you believe *Moses*'s writings? Shall I answer for you, as *Paul* did for *Agrippa*—*I know that*

that thou believest? Would I could!—but what ground is there for this, when you tell us, that you " think yourself at liberty to " consider the history which *Moses* " has given us of the creation " and fall of man, as *the best he* " *could collect from tradition*;" and add—" in my opinion, also, there " are many marks of its being a " very lame account; and, far " from solving the difficulty which " it seems intended to answer, " namely, the introduction of death " and calamity into the world." As for *Paul*, he is to be cashiered as an " inconclusive reasoner;"— and as for his writings, " they " abound with analogies and anti-
" theses,

" theses, on which NO VERY SERI-
" OUS STRESS CAN BE LAID."—In
short, Sir, when we recollect the
manner in which you have treated
the sacred writers in general, and
their *Lord* and *Master* in particular, I think that, ere long, you will
make a *trio* with " *Mr. H.* the *athe-*
" *ist* of *Liverpool*, and his *friend*."
However, Sir, even now there is
much less difference between you,
than you seem to be aware of; for
it appears, from your own writings,
that you are very little, if at all,
removed from those described by
St. Paul, Eph. ii. 12. as *without*
CHRIST—*aliens from the common-*
wealth of Israel—strangers from the
covenants of promise—without hope
—*and*

—*and without God in the world*—
Αθεοι εν κοσμω—literally, *atheists in the world*—*Athei* in mundo. LEUSDEN.

Sir, there is no complimenting and mincing matters on these occasions. The *Christ* which you have described, is not the *Christ* of *Moses* and the Prophets, nor of the Evangelists, and of other New Testament writers. Your God, *in one person*, is not the *Jehovah Aleim* of the Hebrew Scriptures.—How then can you call yourself a Christian believer? and, if not, are you not *an alien from the commonwealth of Israel*—are you not *a stranger from the covenants of promise?*—If so, you can have no
well-

well-grounded *hope*—and if all this be the case, it will stand you in very little stead to say, that *Paul* " reasons inconclusively," when he proves you (as to every intent and purpose that is worth regarding) Αθεος εν κοσμω.

   I am,
    SIR,
     Yours, &c.

LETTER VI.

SIR,

AT the end of my last, I left you in no very pleasant controversy with the *Apostle Paul*. His character is a very extraordinary one, and may not be an unprofitable subject for this my *sixth* address to you. A brief recapitulation of his history, as given us by himself, both before and after his conversion, together with a few plain observations upon it, may do us both good; for you may remember, that he was set *as a pattern to them which should hereafter believe.* 1 Tim. i. 16.

He tells us, *Acts* xxii. 3. that he was a Jew, born in *Tarsus*, a city of *Cilicia*; brought up at *Jerusalem*, at the feet of *Gamaliel*, and taught according to the perfect manner of the law of the fathers, and was zealous towards God, as ye are all (says he to his Jewish hearers) this day. He, after the example of his father, was a Pharisee, chap. xxiii. 6. which was the straitest sect among the Jews, chap. xxvi. 5: they were scrupulous even in the minutest circumstantials of their religion, and on this they rested. They had stripped the law of all its spiritual intendment — the outward letter of the moral law was the rule of their obedience; and an observation

tion of the outward rites of the ceremonial law, was their measure of piety. This was the religion of *Saul*; and so good a man did he think himself, that he was, in his own opinion, *as touching the righteousness which is in the law, blameless*. Phil. iii. 6. He wanted not a better righteousness than his own to justify him: he could, doubtless, say as much of himself as the Pharisee in the temple [*], and thank God that he was not like other men, who had broken the outward letter of the law. Being ignorant of the spirituality of the divine law, both moral and ceremonial, he, under a notion of zeal towards

[*] See *Luke* xviii. 9—15.

God,

God, and in a moft furious rage to maintain the traditions of his fathers, joined moft heartily in the perfecution of the fect of the *Nazarenes*, as the difciples and followers of Chrift were then called, *Acts* xxiv. 5; in fhort, they attacked all his confidence in his own obedience; all his truft in the rites of the ceremonial law was fhaken to the foundation, when they preached the *Crofs of Chrift*, and infifted *that there was no other name given under heaven whereby men could be faved, than that of* Jesus. Acts iv. 12. He was one who was prefent at the ftoning of *Stephen*, Acts vii. 58—And heard him, with his laft breath, *calling upon and saying,* LORD JESUS, RE-CEIVE MY SPIRIT. No doubt but *Saul* (who afterwards was called *Paul*) and all that stood by, were highly offended at this prayer. I question whether Dr. P. Dr. *Price,* Mr. *Lindsey* and Co. could be more offended than they were.

As for *Saul, he made havoc of the church; entering into every house, and haling men and women, committed them to prison, Acts* viii. 3. *And breathing out threatenings and slaughter against the disciples of the Lord*—He procured a plenary commission from the *High Priest, to the synagogues at Damascus,* to arrest, and send bound to *Jerusalem, any of this way, men or women, Acts* ix. 1, 2;

LETTER VI.

1, 2; *for Saul thought that he ought to do many things* (and this among the rest) *contrary to the name of* JESUS, *Acts* xxvi. 9; and particularly to destroy all, who, as *Stephen* had done, *called upon this name* *;
επικαλεμενους

* *To call on the name,* signifies, in the language of Scripture, to *worship,* to *make supplication, prayer,* and *thanksgiving*; see Gen. iv. 26. 1 Kings xviii. 24. Pf. cxvi. 17. Pf. cv. 1. *Jonah* i. 6. & al. freq.; and it is readily agreed, that no *creature* can be the object of it. *Names,* in the Hebrew Bible, were not given arbitrarily, as among us; they always denoted some quality or character of the things or persons on which they were imposed. Hence *Moses* called the name of *Oshea,* who was to subdue the enemies of the *Israelites,* and bring them into the promised land, *Jehoshua,* Numb. xiii. 16.; thus adding one of the divine names יה, the *essence,*

He

ἐπικαλουμενους το Ονομα τȣ͂το, Acts ix. 21.

Saul, armed with his high commission, sets forth for *Damascus*, in

He who Is, the Ὁ ΩΝ, to the word הושׁע from ישׁע *to save*; and thus was he a type or figure in *name*, as well as in *deed*, of the true יהושׁע or *Jesus*, who was so *named of the angel before he was conceived in the womb*, because he was *to save his people from their spiritual enemies, their sins*—Thus doth the name JESUS answer to IMMANUEL—GOD WITH US.

Thus the compound name יהושׁע JEHOSHUA, or JESUS, importing JEHOVAH the SAVIOUR, carries, in itself, a complete answer to all Dr. P.'s profane and absurd ribaldry against the *divinity* and *pre-existence* of OUR GOD AND SAVIOUR JESUS CHRIST. This is He of whom it is written—*Beware of him—obey his voice—provoke him not*—MY NAME IS IN HIM. See Exod. xxiii. 20, 21. and Comp. Pf. ii. 12.

order

order to fulfil it; when, lo! a sudden stop is put to his career, he is himself arrested, convicted, humbled to the dust, changed into another man, as it were.—SAUL the *blasphemer, persecutor*, and *injurious reviler*, Υβριςης (See 1 Tim. i. 13.) is changed into *Paul* the apostle of JESUS CHRIST, *by the commandment of* GOD OUR SAVIOUR, and LORD JESUS CHRIST; and he receives a commission from the LORD HIMSELF, to go *and preach that faith which once he destroyed*, Gal. i. 23. The whole of this transaction is recorded, ACTS ix. 1—19, and Acts xxvi. 12. 9—18, in which last portion of Scripture we find the words of his *commission* recorded; for the plenary fulfilment of which, *he was filled with the* HOLY GHOST, Acts ix. 17, latter part. So that he might well *suppose, that he was not a whit behind the chiefest apostles.* 2 *Cor.* xi. 5.

Such was the man whom you charge with " reasoning incon-
" clusively;"—" whose writings
" (you say) *abound with analogies*
" *and antitheses, on which no very*
" *serious stress can be laid* *." And when certain passages, in these writings, oppose themselves to your *Unitarian* scheme, you say,
" these are not in any *historical*
" *work*, but only incidental expres-
" sions in the epistles of Paul †."

* Letters, p. 159.   † Ibid. p. 118.

As to the term, " incidental ex-"pressions," what can you mean? You quote Eph. iii. 9, and transcribe Col. i. 16, to ver. 20, inclusive, which contains a formal and precise explanation of what was said at ver. 15, viz. *who is the image of the invisible God, the first-born of every creature.* The *former* clause asserting the *divinity* (and consequently the *pre-existence*) of CHRIST (Comp. Heb. i. 3.); the *latter* his holy *humanity* (Comp. Rom. viii. 29.) Then, in the passage which you quote, he explains what he had said, ver. 15, as to both the points, and proves the divinity of *Christ* from *his creating all things*, and being *before all things.*

things.—Then he speaks of him in reference to his holy *humanity*, in which he suffered—*as the beginning, the first-born from the dead—making peace by the blood of his Cross.* So that GOD and MAN IN ONE CHRIST is the grand theme on which this inspired writer delivers his mind, not in *incidental*, transitory *expressions*, though these would have been of undoubted authority (for he *spake in words which were taught him by the Holy Ghost.* 1 Cor. ii. 13.) but in a set, formal, explanatory argument, for *four verses* together.

I am, &c.

LETTER VII.

SIR,

ANalogous to *Col.* i. 15—20. is the text, Phil. ii. 5—11; the *sixth* verse of which you compliment your *Arian* friend, with having translated properly, by rendering αρπαγμον ηγησατο το ειναι ισα Θεω—*did not covet to be honoured as God.* Now, Sir, this is so far from *a proper translation,* as to be no translation at all; it is a sort of paraphrase, which the *Arians* have been forced into, in order to save the throat of their cause; and therefore, why a *Socinian,* or,

as

as you rather chuse to call yourself, an *Unitarian*, should clap the Doctor on the back, with a *macte esto*, is very apparent.

Though " Dr. *Horsley* will not "allow you to know any thing of "*Greek*," and though perhaps his readers may incline to that opinion, yet I think you will vindicate your credit in this respect, if you can fairly prove the above a *proper translation*; that is to say, if you can prove Αρπαγμος is not a substantive, signifying *ipsa rapiendi actio* *, that is, *robbery* ; that ηγεομαι, when applied to the *mind*, does not signify *to think, reckon,*

* *Hedericus*, sub. voc.

esteem ;

esteem; and that το ειναι ινα signifies *to be honoured.*

I advise you against attempting, as some incautiously have done, to construe Αρπαγμον adverbially — as *eagerly, rapaciously,* and the like — for there is no such *adverb* in the Greek language; the verb Αρπαζω gives the nouns Αρπαγμα, Αρπαγη, and Αρπαγμος; but its adverb is Αρπαγιμως, which is not the word made use of, and therefore, we must conclude, not intended by the *apostle.*

" As to the introduction to the
" Gospel of St. *John*, it is not there
" said, that any thing was made
" by Christ, but only by the *Logos,*

"*gos*, which we maintain to be
"the word or power of God,
"which, as it were, resided in
"Christ, to which he ascribed all
"the miracles that he wrought,
"and which there can be no doubt
"(say you) *did* make all things."

You maintain the Logos "to
"be the *word* or *power* of God;"
St. *John* maintains him to *be God*—
the word *was with God, and the*
word was God, says he. Why
do you quibble, and say, that *it is
not there said that any thing was
made by* Christ, but only by the
Logos? The apostle's argument
is to prove the godhead and pre-
existence of that divine person, who
was afterwards *made flesh*, and thus
became

became God and Man in one Christ. Thus he argues:

The word was God. ver. 1.
The word was made flesh,
and dwelt among us. ver. 14.

The irrefragable conclusion to be drawn from these infallible premises is—

Therefore—God was made flesh, and dwelt among us.

Who ever could suppose, that the *Man Christ*, abstractedly considered as to his *human* nature, was the creator of worlds—when that humanity, which he assumed, and which was conceived in the womb of the *Virgin*, certainly did not before exist? But who ever can deny,

deny, if he believes his Bible, that the word—the דבר יהוה as he is called, Gen. xv. 1. (and in divers other paſſages) is a *divine* perſon? that this *divine* perſon appeared frequently, as has been mentioned before in my fourth letter, under a human form, in token or preſage of his future incarnation, and that he was united to the human nature?—and what leſs can we underſtand by St. *John*'s ſaying, ver. 6, *the* word *was made* flesh, *and dwelt among us?*

In ſaying therefore, " there can " be no doubt that the Logos, or " word, *did* make all things, and " reſided in Chriſt," you almoſt talk like a *Chriſtian*. You indeed qualify what you ſay of his " re-
" ſiding

"siding in Christ," with an "as it were," and make the *word* and *power* of GOD convertible terms; thus you save yourself from being thought inconsistent with your own scheme.

The word which we translate *dwelt*, is εσκηνωσεν, a very remarkable expression—literally, *tabernacled*. Thus the dwelling of the divine *Logos* among men in an human body, bears a strong allusion to his formerly *dwelling in the tabernacle* pitched by *Moses*. See *Exod.* xxv. 8. (xxix. 44, 45—6.) *Deut.* xii. 11; in all which passages the word שכן is used, which signifies to *dwell* or *inhabit*, particularly in a *tent* or *tabernacle*.

As

As to your endeavours to overturn the *miraculous birth* of Christ*, at the expence of the cleareft and plaineft teftimonies of the Old and New Teftaments; and certain other attempts to pervert and change the word of God, I leave you to the mafterly fcourge of Dr. *Horsley*; if you do not fmart under this, it is a bad fign for you: as for me, I fhall conclude what I have to fay, by refuming the obfervations which I promifed to make on the character of St. *Paul*; but this muft be the fubject of another letter.

I am, &c.

* Here Dr. P.'s allies the *Mahommedans* defert him. See *Sale*'s KORAN, chap. iii. chap. iv. chap. xix.

LETTER VIII.

SIR,

I PURPOSE to begin this letter, with obferving fome particulars in the hiftory of St. *Paul*.

Before his converfion he was, doubtlefs, like the reft of his apoftate countrymen, *a Unitarian*, a defpifer and reviler of CHRIST, a rejecter of his *facrifice* of atonement, of his *righteoufnefs* for juftification, of his *fpirit* for fanctification, of his *interceffion* for prefervation, and in fhort, of his whole work of *redemption*. All this arofe from that *vail which was upon his heart,*

heart, so that he understood not the Scriptures, which *were red in the synagogues every sabbath-day.* (Acts xv. 21.) He was therefore proud, self-righteous, ignorant, and unbelieving. He thought himself, *as touching the law, blameless* (in every sense of the word); he was quite heart-whole, and nothing could prove such a *stumbling-block,* as the preaching salvation through the atonement and righteousness of the crucified Jesus. He was seeking righteousness by the works of the law: the letter of the *moral* law bore him out against all accusations of his conscience; the strict observance of the *ceremonial* law, exalted him as a great faint in his own eyes; he was fortified by something like Horace's *Murus aheneus*;

Nil conscire sibi, nullâ pallescere culpâ.

Hence his thorough enmity to the whole work of Christ, to his *person* and *offices*, and, of course, to all who set him forth as the hope and salvation of *Israel*.

In this state of mind, could he have written his epistles? or, if *any one else* had written them, could he, think you, Sir, have understood them? What would he have made of " *There is none righ-* " *teous, no, not one; therefore by the* " *deeds of the law shall no flesh be* " *justified:*

"justified: for by the law is the
"knowledge of sin. But now the
"RIGHTEOUSNESS OF GOD WITH-
"OUT THE LAW *is manifested, being
"witnessed by the law and the pro-
"phets: even the righteousness of
"God which is by faith of* JESUS
"CHRIST, *unto all, and upon all
"them that believe: for there is no
"difference: for all have sinned and
"come short of the glory of God;
"being justified freely by his grace,
"through the redemption that is in*
"CHRIST JESUS, *whom God hath
"set forth to be a* PROPITIATION
"THROUGH FAITH IN HIS BLOOD,
"*to declare his righteousness for the
"remission of sins that are past,
"through the forbearance of God.*——
"To

" To declare, I say, at this time his
" righteousness, that he might be
" just, and the justifier of him which
" believeth in Jesus. Where is
" boasting then? it is excluded.
" By what law? of works? Nay,
" but by the law of faith. There-
" fore we conclude, that a man is
" justified by faith, without the deeds
" of the law."

He is " an inconclusive rea-
" soner"— says *Saul*, the Pharisee.

Again.—*By one man sin entered
into the world, and death by sin;
and so, death passed upon all men, for
that all have sinned; as by one man's
disobedience many were made sinners,
so, by the obedience of one, shall many*

be made righteous. Moreover, the law entered that the offence might abound. But where sin abounded, grace did much more abound. That as sin reigned unto death, even so might grace reign, through righteousness, unto eternal life, by JESUS CHRIST OUR LORD.

The first man Adam *was made a living soul, the last* Adam *a quickening spirit.*

The first *man is of the earth earthy, the* second *man the* LORD *from Heaven.*

" This is no *historical* account, " it is only *casual epistolary* writing "—No serious stress is to be laid " upon it"—says our *Cilician.*

" To

"*To the church of God which is at Corinth, to them that are sanctified in Christ Jesus, called to be saints, with all that in every place* CALL UPON THE NAME of JESUS CHRIST OUR LORD *." Comp. *Pf.* xcix. 6.

"O shocking! What blasphemy! Why this is downright *idolatry!*"—What! *pray* † to "a mere man, a fallible, peccable, weak, human being, like ourselves! I'll get a commission from the High Priest; I'll hale men and women to prison, and when they are put to death, I'll give my voice against them" — quoth *Saul,* the *Unitarian.*

* 1 Cor. i. 2.   † See before, p. 51, note.

Such doubtless must have been the observations of Paul *before* his conversion, had such writings as his *own epistles* been laid before him. What views he had of these matters after his conversion, must be considered in another letter.

I am, &c.

LETTER IX.

SIR,

I COME now to consider the sentiments of *Paul,* after his conversion: that this was effected by supernatural agency, none can doubt, who believe the apostle's own account of the matter. *Acts* ix. 1—18.

My present business is to consider his sentiments, with respect to the *law* and the *gospel*. That, before his conversion, he saw no farther than the outward letter of the law, we must conclude, from his imagining himself, *as touching the righteousness*

righteousness which is in the law, BLAMELESS, or *unblameable,* αμεμϕͅος. He thought, therefore, that he wanted not a better righteousness than his own for his justification. But when it pleased God to open his eyes, so that he saw that the *law was spiritual,* and reached to the very inmost thoughts, intents, desires, and affections of the heart —he then was apprized of his guilt and danger. He then saw that, as *many as are of the works of the law are under the curse,* i. e. under the malediction and condemnation of that holy dispensation, which says, *Cursed is every one that continueth not in all things which are written in the book of the law*

law to do them, Deut. xxvii. 26 *. *I had not known sin* (says he) *but by the law; for I had not known lust, except the law had said thou shalt not covet. But sin taking occasion by the commandment, wrought in me all manner of concupiscence. For without the law,* (i. e. without a spiritual view of it within his conscience) *sin was dead.—For I was alive without the law once, but when the commandment came, sin revived, and I died. Rom.* vii. 7—9.

Here, I grant, are figurative expressions, but they are so apposite, so adapted, so explanatory of the subject, as to be well worth

* Comp. *Gal.* iii. 10.

notice.

notice. By a fine *prosopopeia*, he speaks of sin, while it lay quiet, and gave him no disturbance, as of a dead person who can hurt nobody; but when the law, which *is the strength of sin* (as he expresses it, 1 Cor. xv. 56.) i. e. that which gives it a power to torment and wound the conscience, and bind over to punishment, *came*, i. e. was revealed to me in its accusing and condemning power—*sin revived*—like one raised from the dead, to all the functions of life and power; appeared in its full force to condemn and destroy, *and I died*—all my hopes were blasted—my confidence gone, and the dismal sentence of eternal death

took

took place within me. He then *knew* *, *that in him, that is, in his flesh*, or natural self, notwithstanding all his boasted blamelessness, *there dwelt no good thing*; and he was reduced to cry out, in the anguish of his soul, *Wretched man that I am! who shall deliver me from the body of this death?* Rom. vii. 24. As he thus saw the spirituality and holiness of the *moral* law, he could find no relief till he also saw the end, purpose, and design of the *ceremonial* law, and that it was to lead him through the *sign* to the *thing signified*—from the *shadows* to the *substance*—that with-

* Rom. vii. 18.

out *shedding blood there was no remission; that the blood of bulls and goats could not take away sin**, as pertaining to the conscience, *for then they would have ceased to be offered*, i. e. they would not have needed repetition, *because that the worshippers once purged should have had no more conscience of sins*†. This he felt most deeply; he had been of the *straitest sect, a Pharisee*, had attended constantly on the temple-worship, but all this gave him no comfort; he had been taught at the feet of *Gamaliel* — he *profited in the Jews religion above many his equals in his own nation*, but

* Heb. ix. 9.   † Ibid. x. 2.

all

all would not do—he could not extract one grain of comfort from all his wisdom, knowledge, learning, or pharisaical holiness and righteousness, of which he once thought so highly; but when it *pleased God to reveal his son in him**, then the vail was taken from his heart, his ignorance and unbelief fell from his mind, as the scales had once fallen from his eyes—and he now saw that CHRIST *is the end of the law for righteousness to every one that believeth*; and in the midst of his doleful lamentation, *Wretched man, who shall deliver me!* &c. he is enabled to say, *I thank God through* JESUS CHRIST OUR LORD †;

* Gal. i. 16. † Rom. vii. 25.
—the

—the law of the SPIRIT OF LIFE IN CHRIST JESUS *hath made me free from the law of sin and death* *.

Now, Sir, mark the sequel:—He no longer joined his old brethren the *Pharisees*, in *rejecting* † and *despising* the *man of sorrows*; he no longer regarded him as a " *mere man*, naturally weak, fallible, peccable, ignorant like one of us." —But looked upon him as *the second man, the Lord from heaven, the Lord of glory* ‡, *the brightness* § (απαυγασμα, the effulgence, splendor) *of the glory* of the DEITY ‖, and the ex-

* Rom. viii. 2.   † Iſ. liii. 3.
‡ 1 Cor. ii. 8.   § Heb. i. 3.

‖ Χαρακτηρ της υποστασεως αυτε.—Character substantiæ ejus. *Leusd.* See *Parkhurst* Gr. and Eng. Lexicon, Χαρακτηρ.

press

press image of his person.—*God, who commanded the light to shine out of darkness*, had shined into his heart, giving him the light of the knowledge of the glory of God in the face or person* (εν προσωπω) *of* JESUS CHRIST. He now understood how Christ was *David's Lord*, and *David's son*, and that in *Him dwelt* ALL THE FULLNESS OF THE GODHEAD BODILY (σωματικως); not only *effectually*, as God is said to dwell in *good men*, but *substantially* and *personally*, as the soul within the body.

Again.—*Paul* laid aside his *Unitarianism*; and when he blesses the

---

* 2 Cor. iv. 6.

Corinthians, he says, *The grace of our* Lord Jesus Christ, *and the love of* God, *and the communion of the* Holy Ghost *be with you all**; — thus copying, in evangelical terms, the manner of blessing in the name of Jehovah under the law. Numb. vi. 23—26.——*On this wise shall ye bless the children of Israel:*

> Jehovah bless thee and keep thee.
>
> Jehovah make his face to shine upon thee, and be gracious unto thee.
>
> Jehovah lift up his countenance

---

* 2 Cor. xiii. 14.

upon

upon thee, and give thee peace *.

This

---

* The learned bishop *Patrick*, in his comment on these verses, Numb. vi. 24—6, remarks, that " the repetition of this name " *three* times, in these three verses, and that with a different accent (as *R. Menachem* observes) hath made the Jews themselves think there is some mystery in it: which we understand, though they do not. For it may well be looked upon by us, as having respect to the *three* persons in the blessed Trinity, who are One GOD, from whom all blessings flow to us. 2 Cor. xiii. 14.

This mystery, as *Luther* wisely expresses it (upon Pf. v.) is here *occultè infinuatum*, "secretly insinuated," though not plainly revealed. And it is not hard to shew, if this were a place for it, how properly God the Father may be said *to bless* and *keep us*;

and

This subject must be pursued in another letter; in the mean time
I am, &c.

and God the Son to be *gracious unto us*; and God the Holy Ghost to *give us peace*.

Hermannus Witsius, Misc. Sacr. Lib. 2. Dissertat. II. p. 518, more largely to the same purpose, on this Scripture, says:

Maximè μυστηριωδης, est *trina* nominis *Jehovæ* repetitio: neque rejicienda R. *Menachem* nota de trina accentuum in eadem voce variatione: quæ quid convenientius significari potest, quam adoranda divinarum personarum in una Deitate Trinitas, unde, velut ex perenni fonte, omnis in nos benedictio derivatur? Confer 2 Cor. xiii. 14. Apoc. i. 4—6.

Prima pericopa. BENEDICAT TIBI JEHOVAH ET CUSTODIAT TE—percommode refertur ad PATREM, de quo Paulus scribit, Eph. i. 3. *Benedictus esto Deus, &* PATER *Domini nostri Jesu Christi*, qui BENEDIXIT
nobis.

LETTER IX.

nobis omni spirituali benedictione in Christo. Et cui Christus ipse dicit. John xvii. 11. PATER *Sancte*, SERVA *eos per nomen tuum.*

Altera pericopa. FACIAT JEHOVAH UT LUCEAT FACIES SUA TIBI, ET GRATIAM FACIAT TIBI.—Ad CHRISTUM pertinet, qui est LUX MUNDI, & *coelestis Hierosolymae.* Apoc. xxi. 23. *Cujus facies splendet uti sol.* Apoc. i. 16. *In cujus facie est lux notitiae gloriae Dei.* 2 Cor. iv. 6. In ¡quo plenissimè completur illa sapientissimi Regis paroemia. Prov. xvi. 15. *In lucida facie Regis vita est, ejusque benevolentia est velut nubes pluviae Serotinae*; in quo denique sunt *supereminentes opes gratiae.* Eph. ii. 7.

Ultima pericopa. ATTOLLAT JEHOVAH FACIEM SUAM ERGA TE, ET APPONAT TIBI PACEM, quum notat applicationem gratiae, & communicationem pacis ac gaudii, commodè applicatur SPIRITUI SANCTO, per quem *regnum Dei* nobis est *justitia, & pax, & gaudium.* Rom. xiv. 17.

LETTER X.

SIR,

IN my last, was considered the alteration which passed in the sentiments of *Paul*, with regard to the *Person of* CHRIST: full as great was the change wrought in his mind concerning *the offices of Christ*.

The name CHRIST, we know, signifies *anointed*, and he is called *the* LORD's CHRIST, Luke ii. 26, which is his title. *Psalm* ii. 2.

The משיחים, or *anointed ones*, under the law, were *Kings*. See 2 Sam.

Sam. i. 21; *Priests*, See Lev. x. 7; and *Prophets*, 1 Kings xix. 16: they were anointed to their office by pouring oil on their heads.

Paul saw, after his conversion, that all these three offices had their ultimate designation, and all met in CHRIST, and that He was the great משיח, Χριςος—anointed KING, PRIEST, and PROPHET; *his understanding being opened to understand the Scriptures, and all things that were written in the law of Moses**, and in *the Prophets,* and in *the Psalms*, concerning that JESUS whom he had once reviled and persecuted. He well knew who

---

* Comp. Luke xxiv. 44, 45.

was meant by that *King** who was to be *set on Sion, the mountain of God's holiness*; who that אן, *Lord*, was, to whom JEHOVAH said, *Sit thou at my right hand, till I make thine enemies thy footstool*†; to whom JEHOVAH swore, *thou art a Priest for ever, after the order of Melchizedec*; in whom the regal and sacerdotal offices were united. Comp. Gen. xiv. 18, with Heb. vii. 1—3.

Paul, any more than *Peter* or *Stephen*, had now no doubt whom *Moses* meant, by that prophet whom JEHOVAH *promised to raise up like unto him*, who should speak his words to the people. Comp.

* Pf. ii. 6.
† Pf. cx. 1, 4, with Heb. x. 13.

Deut.

Deut. xviii. 15, 18, 19, with Acts iii. 22, 23, and Acts vii. 37.

I think, Sir, you will allow that a *King* must have subjects to govern, a *Priest* something to offer for sins, and a *Prophet* something to reveal and foretel.

Let us hear what is said of Christ as a *King*, Mic. v. 2. His goings *forth have been from of old*; מימי עולם, from the days of eternity; and If. ix. 7, of the increase of his government and peace there shall be no end, upon the throne of *David*, and upon his kingdom, to order it and to establish it with judgment and with justice, from henceforth even for ever. — See this applied to *Jesus*, Luke i. 31—33.

Does

Does this imply that Christ was a *mere man*—what *mere man* had his goings forth from everlasting? Comp. Mic. v. 2, with Matt. ii. 6. What *mere man* can reign *for ever?* But unto the Son he saith, Pf. xlv. 6, 7, *Thy throne, O* God, *is for ever and ever; the sceptre of thy kingdom is a right sceptre; thou haſt loved righteousneſs, and hated wickedneſs; therefore God, even thy God, hath anointed thee with the oil of gladneſs above thy fellows.* Comp. Heb. i. 8, 9.

And again:—Pſ. cii. 24, latter part, and ver. 25—27. Comp. Heb. i. 10. 12.

And can it be poſſible for any one to think, that *Paul*, after his converſion,

conversion, could consider Christ as a *mere man*, when he so understood and so applied these Scriptures, as to evince the contrary? and if not, can we be justified in differing from him?

Again.—He calls Christ the great *High Priest*, as well as the *blessed Apostle of our profession*, Heb. iii. 1, and tells us, that *every High Priest is ordained to offer gifts and sacrifices; wherefore it is of necessity that this man have somewhat also to offer* *. And what was this? —no less than the *sacrifice of himself* †.—Thus fulfilling the law by his obedience unto death, and

* Heb. viii. 3. † Ibid. ix. 26.

proving himself, in purpose, design, and efficacy, the great antitype of the legal priesthood, sacrifices, and oblations, which were offered under the *Mosaic* dispensation. Thus Christ *died for our sins, according to the Scriptures* *; he suffered, the *just for the unjust, that he might bring us to God* †; and having BY HIMSELF *purged our sins, for ever, sat down on the right-hand of the Majesty on high*. Heb. i. 3.

When we are told, that he was *made sin for us*, or a *sin-offering* (for αμαρτια, like the Hebrew חטאת, signifies both the *sin*, and the *sin-offering*) it implies, that the sins of

---

* 1 Cor. xv. 3. † 1 Pet. iii. 18.

those whom he represented, as in the sin-offering under the law, were *imputed* to him, or, as If. liii. 6, *laid upon him*; (Comp. Lev. xvi. 21.) and that he made an atonement, satisfaction, propitiation, and reconciliation; this is received by faith into the conscience, and is the only thing that can satisfy it, or give the sinner any true hope of deliverance from everlasting death. So *Paul* found it; and so, Sir, a time will come, when you would give the whole world for one saving glimpse of this *great mystery of godliness*. The *imputation* of our sins to CHRIST, and the *imputation* of the merit of *his blood and righteousness* to us, is

one

one of those great gospel-truths *, which discriminate it from every other system of religion; it was the grand theme of *Paul*'s sermons and epistles — all his pharisaical

* This the law, which *was a figure for the time then present*, taught throughout. See, for instance, Lev. i. 4, where the man who brought his burnt-offering to the door of the tabernacle, as a sacrifice for sin, was to *put his hand upon the head of the burnt-offering*, and, saith the text, *it shall be accepted for him, to make atonement for him*. The putting his hand on the head of the offering was an emblem of a *transfer* made of the offerer's sins to the sacrifice; its being *accepted to make atonement*, or expiation, *for him*, signified, that the victim's expiatory death was accepted instead of the offerer's, and *imputed* to him for the acceptance of his person, and for the expiation of his sins.

pride was laid in the duſt—his learning, his privileges, his goodneſs and righteouſneſs, which he once thought ſo highly of, were all thought of as nothing, nay, worſe than nothing; for he ſays, enumerating the ſeveral grounds of confidence which once he boaſted of—*What things were gain to me, thoſe I counted loſs for* CHRIST*; *yea, doubtleſs, and I count all things but loſs for the excellency of the knowledge of* CHRIST JESUS MY LORD : *for whom I have ſuffered the loſs of all things, and do count them but dung* (σκυβαλα) *that I may win* CHRIST, *and be found* IN HIM

* Phil. iii. 7, 10.

(N. B.)

(N. B.) not having MY OWN. RIGHTEOUSNESS *which is of the law, but* (N. B.) *that which is through the faith of Christ, the righteousness which is of God by faith* *.

* Εμην την δικαιοσυνην την εκ νομω, my righteousness *which is of law,* my own *legal righteousness.* He saw that no obedience of his own to the divine law, either *moral* or *ceremonial,* could justify him; by the *former* was the *knowledge of sin,* and *that* sin could not be taken away by the *latter,* but only by that to which it pointed. Thus was *the law a schoolmaster to bring him to* CHRIST, *that he might be justified by faith,* Gal. iii. 24. He knew enough of the law and of himself, to know, that it was *the ministration of death, and that by the deeds of the law no flesh could be justified,* Rom. iii. 20. Therefore, says he, *Gal.* vi. 14, GOD *forbid that I should glory,* save in the cross of our LORD JESUS CHRIST!

In.

In all this, *Paul* could not think of CHRIST as a *mere man*; for *no man can redeem his brother, or give to God his atonement*—כפרו. Pſ. xlix. 7. A *mere man* can, therefore, only ſuffer, or obey, for himſelf, not for others.

Leaving this to your conſideration,

I am, &c.

LETTER XI.

SIR,

LET us now consider the views which *Paul* had of Christ in the office of a *prophet*. The prophets of old revealed the mind of GOD, as discovered to them by the Holy Spirit. *Moses* not only revealed things to *come*, but also things *past*, such as the creation of the world, the fall of man, and the general history of the church for many ages afterwards. Your notion, that *Moses* " *collected* these " things by *tradition*," is very curious, when you are told, 2 Tim. iii.

iii. 16, *that all Scripture is* GIVEN *by inspiration of God; and that holy men of old spake as they were moved by the Holy Ghost.* 2 Pet. i. 21 ; and when we see that this prerogative of revealing things *past*, is one grand criterion, to distinguish between the true ALEIM of *Israel*, and the false ones, the *idols* of the heathen. *Let them bring forth, and shew what shall happen, let them shew the former things what they be, that we may consider them. Who hath declared from the beginning, that we may know? and before time, that we may say, he is righteous? &c* *.

However, Sir, there is a great difference between you and *Paul*,

---

* If. xli. 22.

in respect to *Moses*' account of the *fall*; he treats it as fully accounting for the introduction of sin and death into the world; you call it "a *lame account,*" and not adequate to this purpose.—*Paul* lays it as the grand basis of all his arguments, for redemption by Christ, whom he calls the second *Adam,* and says, that the first *Adam was the figure of him that was to come.* You, Sir (forgetting that *Paul* spake, * *not in the words which man's wisdom teacheth, but which the* HOLY GHOST *teacheth, comparing spiritual things with spiritual,* i. e. one revealed truth with another)

* 1 Cor. ii. 13.

boast

boast of having the writings of *Moses* before you, as well as *Paul*, and speak as if you were as well able to judge of them as he was, nay better, for you style him " an " inconclusive reasoner," reject *his* interpretations, and advance *your own*. And such they are, as even Dr. *Price* *, your *Arian* friend, " and others, may well be stag-" gered at." You say yourself, that you " believe your opinions no-" vel †, and a step beyond what
"other

---

* Letters, p. 164.

† The *Doctor's* opinions may be *novel*, in the sense here mentioned; but the notion of a *sinner's* approaching his OFFENDED MAKER, without an *atonement by blood*, is as old as the days of *Adam's* first-born, *Cain*.

Comp.

"other *Socinians* have gone." It is to be hoped, that, ere long, you will *stagger* yourself, as was the case of the famous *Earl* of *Rochester*; who, having made a speech in favour of *Atheism*, so eloquently, as to *stagger* the company which was with him at a tavern; when he got home, he began to reflect on what he had done, and was so filled with remorse, that he past the night in the utmost disquiet of mind, overwhelmed with shame and sorrow; and this is said to have laid the first foundation of his repentance.

Comp. Gen. iv. 3—5, with Heb. xi. 4. *Cain* may be looked upon as the *tutelar saint* of the *Socinians* and *Deists*.

But

But to return.—However, before his conversion, *Paul* might view CHRIST as *a deceiver**, as the other *Pharisees* did; yet after, he certainly beheld him as that *Prophet which was to come, John* vi. 14; even as the MESSIAH, of whom it is written, *Behold my servant whom I uphold, mine elect in whom my soul delighteth: I have put my spirit upon him, he shall bring forth judgment to the Gentiles*, &c. Comp. Matt. xii. 18, Matt. iii. 17, and Matt. xvii. 5. And again, speaking by the prophet *Isaiah*, he saith (chap. lxi. 1.) the spirit of ADONI JEHOVAH, is upon 'me; (Comp.

* Matt. xxvii. 63.

Matt. iii. 16.) because JEHOVAH *hath anointed me to preach good tidings unto the meek,* &c. to the end of ver. 3; and comp: Luke iv. 17—21. Nor did he view him as a *mere man* even in this part of his character; but as *having the spirit without measure* *; as him *in whom were hidden all the treasures of wisdom and knowledge* †, yea, as the *very wisdom and power of God* ‡.

You, Sir, tell us, that he was " a *mere man,* naturally weak and " fallible as other men §;" and this, though it be written, Is. vii. 14. (in allusion, doubtless, to *the seed of the woman,* Gen. iii. 15.)

* John iii. 34. † Col. ii. 3.
‡ 1 Cor. i. 24. § Letters, p. 171.

Behold

Behold a virgin shall conceive and bear a Son, and shall call his name עמנואל—*Omnu-al*, or, if you please, *Immanuel*, which, being interpreted, is, GOD WITH US. Comp. Matt. i. 22, 23. The manner of his *conception* is revealed, ver. 18. And *Luke* records the whole history of his miraculous *conception*, chap. i. 35; his wondrous *birth*, foretold by an angel, ver. 26—31, and celebrated by choirs of *the heavenly host, praising God, and saying, Glory be to God in the highest, and on earth peace, good-will towards men!*—and all this, that " a mere " man, naturally weak, fallible, " peccable, as other men," was born into the world!—Sir, you believe

lieve a *great deal*; I hope, *more* than most people pretend to : however, it is for us to quote the Scriptures; be it yours to deny or pervert them, if you please, as may best destroy their evidence against you.

I am, &c.

LETTER XII.

SIR,

I NOW enter upon the design I had in saying so much of the *Apostle Paul*, both before and after his conversion. It was this—to set before you by *example*, which is stronger than *precept*, the real condition which you yourself are in; in hopes, that, if what has been said does not affect your *head*, as a wise *scholar*, it may in some measure affect your *conscience* as a *lost sinner*. You seem by your writings to *have a zeal of God**; so had

* Rom. x. 2.

Saul,

Saul, but it was *not according to knowledge*; no more is yours, the Bible being judge of you, as it was of him. He, *being ignorant of God's righteousness, went about to establish his own righteousness* *; so do you. He did not *submit to the righteousness of God*, or to the *righteousness of faith*, as it is called, Rom. ix. 30, or *the righteousness which is of God, which is through the faith of Christ*. Phil. iii. 9. This is exactly your case; your confidence is placed in some personal obedience of your own. *He was alive without the law* †; he saw not that it required a sinless obe-

---

* Rom. x. 3.   † Ibid. vii. 9.

dience

dience in thought, word, and deed, on pain of death—that therefore he neither had, nor could avoid its curse, by any obedience which he could pay it. This *you* see nothing of, and therefore *you* are *alive* in your own conceit; you want not a better obedience than your own, to *constitute* you righteous before God *.

He *verily thought with himself that he ought to do many things contrary to the name of* JESUS †.

You have actually done almost as many things *contrary to the name of Jesus,* as you have written pages.

---

* Rom. v. 19; where the word καταςαθη-σονται is very remarkable. See Rev. iii. 17.

† Acts xxvi. 9.

He was *a blasphemer* *, though he knew it not; so are *you,* as far one of the greatest this land has produced, as you "go beyond what other *Socinians* have gone †."

He was a *persecutor*.

You may perhaps think, that the professions which you ‡ make of *tolerancy*, must exempt you from this charge; but if your attempts to promote a repeal of the test-acts had succeeded, and by degrees we had had a *Socinian,* or, if you chuse to call it, an *Unitarian* parliament—an *Unitarian* army and navy—how long should we have kept a *Trinitarian* liturgy—a *Trini-*

* 1 Tim. i. 13.   † Letters, p. 164.
‡ Letters, p. 68.

tarian establishment? or how long should we have been suffered, with the *Apostles* and first *Christians*, to worship, or, to express it in Scripture language, *to call on the name of Jesus Christ, both their Lord and ours* *? The zeal which you shew in your writings to make proselytes to your opinions, gives us but small hopes of your tolerating, what you have undertaken to prove to be *blasphemy* and *idolatry*, if once it were " in your power to " be intolerant †."

And I do verily believe, that if that divine person, who appeared to *Saul* in the way to Damascus,

---

* 1 Cor. i. 2. † Letters, p. 68.

should graciously pity your *ignorance* and *unbelief**, as he did his—should meet and stop you in your way by the power of his grace—and you were to ask with *Saul*, "*Who art thou, Lord?*" he would answer *you*, as he did *him*, "I am "Jesus, *whom thou perfecutest.*" For if to destroy his character, to vilify his person, to annihilate his offices, and to engage others to follow your example, be not deserving of this charge, I know not what is.

He was *injurious*—Ὑβριϛης, *injuriosus, contumeliosus*. In Rom. i. 30, we find Θεοϛυγεις, *haters of God*,

* 1 Tim. i. 13.

joined with ὙΒρισας, *injurious revilers*, and they are fit company for each other. That *Saul* was a *hater of God*, is clear from his hatred to Christ; for our Lord declares, *John* xv. 23. *He that hateth me, hateth my father also.* Such as he *was*, such *are* you; hence his and your *contumelies* against Christ. The only foundation on which a sinful creature can love an Holy God, is that, which *Saul* and *you* may be called equal strangers to, and is recorded, 1 John iv. 10. " *Herein is love, not that we loved* " *God, but that he loved us, and sent* " *his Son to be the* PROPITIATION " (Ιλασμον, *a propitiatory victim*— " a *sacrifice for sin*—as the word is

I " used

"used by the LXX for חטאת, *Ezek.* xliv. 27.) *for our sins.*" This *Saul* denied, and so do *you.* "*The divine Being* (say you *) is declared to be as merciful in the Old Testament as in the New, and that without reference to any future event."—*Saul* did all this *in ignorance and unbelief* †; how far the parallel holds here, I presume not to determine, this must be left to the searcher of hearts.—You once knew better, *Saul* did not.

You once was "‡ a *Trinitarian*, then you passed to *high Arianism*, from this to your friend Dr.

---

* Letters, p. 157.   † 1 Tim. i. 13.
‡ Letters, p. 101.
"*Price's*

"*Price's low Arianism*, and from this to *Socinianism*, even of the lowest kind; in which Christ is considered as a mere man, the son of *Joseph* and *Mary*, and naturally as peccable as *Moses*, or any other prophet."—You express it, p. 171, "Naturally as weak, as fallible, and as peccable as other men."—And as to his understanding "all preceding prophecies, we are no where told, that he was inspired with that knowledge; and therefore he might apply them as his countrymen generally did" (*i. e.* misapply them); "and as we perceive that the apostles, who were likewise prophets, did afterwards."

If by *afterwards* be meant, when, after his resurrection, *he opened their understandings, that they might understand the Scriptures*—it is contrary to fact—No one instance of it can be produced. See *Luke* xxiv. 45,

But the true meaning of these horrid imputations of ignorance of the Scriptures to CHRIST and his *Apostles*, is, to remove their authority out of the way of the *Socinian* scheme, which otherwise must be destroyed.—Ask yourself, Sir, if this be not so?—Let me take my leave of you for this time, with recommending your assertion with respect to "CHRIST's not be-
"ing inspired with the knowledge
"of all preceding prophecies," to
your

your own confideration, on the footing of what is faid of him, *If.* xi. 2. *And the Spirit of the Lord fhall reft upon him, the fpirit of wifdom and underftanding, the fpirit of counfel and might, the fpirit of knowledge and of the fear of the Lord, and fhall make him of quick underftanding in the fear of the Lord.*

Again.—He faid to the *eleven, when gathered together, and them that were with them* *,

Thefe are the words which I fpake unto you, WHILE I WAS YET WITH YOU, *that all things muft be fulfilled, which were written in the law of Mofes, and in the Prophets,*

---

* Luke xxiv. 44.

and in the Psalms, concerning me. How could this be, if he did not, WHILE HE WAS YET WITH THEM, *understand all preceding prophecies?*

    I am,

      SIR, &c.

LETTER XIII.

SIR,

IN my laſt, I tranſcribed ſome of your own account of your great *verſatility*, in your religious opinions; to which I muſt add ſomething that we meet with, *Letters*, p. 168, where you ſay of yourſelf—

"So far from having much
"fondneſs for the opinions that I
"received from my education, I
"have gone on changing, though
"always in one direction, from
"the time that I began to think
"for myſelf, to the preſent day,
"and

"and I will not pretend to say
"when my creed will be fixed."

I read of some, who are *ever learning, and never able to come to the knowledge of the truth*, 2 Tim. iii. 7; and the next verse says, that as *Jannes and Jambres withstood Moses, so do these resist the truth, men of corrupt minds, reprobate concerning the faith.* Of others, Eph. iv. 14, who are *like children, carried away with every wind of doctrine by the slight of men, and cunning craftiness whereby they lie in wait to deceive.* Do you not, Sir, perceive something in the above descriptions, which bears a strong resemblance to that which you have given of yourself? You

have

have been *ever learning,* but " you " have not fixed your creed;" therefore, upon your own shewing, you have not yet come to the knowledge of any thing on which you can rely as *truth.*

You have been carried away by *every wind of doctrine,* to almost every point of the compass, and yet you are not *fixed.*—Alas, Sir, the true reason of all this is, that your " changes have been all in " one direction;" namely, that of establishing the empire of your *reason,* against that of revelation. You forget, that *no prophecy of the Scripture is of any private interpretation; for the prophecy came not in old time by the will of man, but holy*

holy men of God spake as they were moved by the Holy Ghost;—and that the *natural man,* Ψυχικος Ανθρωπος, the mere *sensual* man, who lives by *sense,* and not by *faith;* such a one, be he ever so *wise in his own eyes,* or *prudent in his own sight*—be he ever so worldly-wise or learned—*receiveth not the things of the Spirit of God, for they are* foolishness unto him, *because they are spiritually discerned.* See 1 *Cor.* ii. 7—16. Hence, instead of humbly submitting your reason, as it is most reasonable you should, to the word of God, you are, with an *inveniam viam aut faciam,* endeavouring to make the word of God submit to your reason.

son. Your reason, which is designed to be the *scholar*, usurps the place of the *teacher*. If you have met with opinions, which are above your apprehension, you have quarrelled with them, and left them for something more flattering to your vain opinion of your own wisdom :—this brought you from *Trinitarianism* to *high Arianism*—thence to *low Arianism*—thence into *Socinianism*—and thence into something lower still ;—thus have you advanced in an inverted *ratio* very near *Deism*, and when you have gotten thither, you will no longer be thwarted by Scripture - testimony; your *creed* will be fixed, on the wise determinations of *Collins*,

lins, Tindal, Bolingbroke, &c.; and then, by the help of your own *materialism* and *philosophical necessity,* it is not impossible but that, with *Hobbes, Spinosa,* and Mr. H. of *Liverpool,* you will sit down at last a complete *Atheist*; and then, Sir, you will have done with all creeds whatsoever, and, by the way, save yourself a great deal of trouble.

You mention " the *great teacher* " *Death,* and the scenes that will " follow it;" and say, that " in all " probability you must wait till " the arrival of these for farther " light." Death, and the scenes that will follow it, will certainly *fix your creed,* so that you can change no more; but, as *the tree falls*

falls so it must lie; and a most awful confideration it is! feeing that death muft fix your ftate for ever—though now you do not *believe* that you have a *foul**, yet then you will *know* that that you have one; and that, if *that foul* be not cleanfed from the guilt of all its fins in the blood of *Jefus Chrift* †, it had been better for you that you *had never been born*.—This farther light will then break in upon you, whether you will or not, for then fhall you *know even as you are known*. 1 Cor. xiii. 12.

But before this, there is an awful fcene approaching, and how

* Letters, p. 72.
† 1 John i. 7. Rev. i. 5.

near it may be, God only knoweth! I mean, Sir, a DEATH-BED, where every outward comfort muſt fail us—all earthly enjoyment vaniſh—nothing left to ſupport—and every dream of creature-happineſs be exchanged for the ſad reality of pain and ſickneſs. Nothing can counteract the miſery of this, but a well-grounded hope of future happineſs in a better world. By this I mean, a hope, or expectation, in which we are warranted to reſt, by evidence which is fully compe- tent to the ſtreſs we lay upon it.

Let us then ſuppoſe, that (added to our bodily afflictions) our minds no longer ſatisfied, our conſciences no longer ſilenced, with the things

of

of time and sense, are filled with terror and dread of a judgment to come. We see, as it were, an holy GOD whom we have offended, an holy law which we have broken;—how shall the breach be healed? how shall our peace be made?—Our imaginations, which, when we were in health, could please us with their excursions into various systems of self-confidence, are now confined within, and gather terror from what passes there.—Our reason would present us comfort from its own conclusions; but we shall find its premises are false—it will exalt MERCY at the expence of JUSTICE—and, being biassed by our wishes, flatter us with knowing, what none but Heaven itself can teach

teach — how *mercy and truth can meet together* — how *righteousness and peace can kiss each other* *.— But in all in vain!

The *sting of death is sin; the strength of sin is the law*. The *law worketh wrath* †—it reveals to us the *wrath of God against all unrighteousness and ungodliness of men* ‡ —it lays us under *a curse*, but cannot deliver us from it. The more we call in aid our own obedience to satisfy it, the faster it binds us over to condemnation. All is imperfect, short of what the law requires, and therefore sinful; *for all unrighteousness is sin*. 1 John v. 17.

* Pſ. lxxxv. 10.   † Rom. iv. 15.
‡ Rom. i. 18.   § Gal. iii. 10.

But

But when we view our actual transgressions, which are *more in number than the hairs of our head**, then *our hearts will fail us*, and we shall be like *David*, Pf. lxxxviii. 8. where he says, *I am shut up; I cannot come forth.* So Paul, *Gal.* iii. 22. *The Scripture hath concluded all under sin*—συνεκλεισεν—*shut them up together, as in a prison.*

Now, Sir, suppose yourself in this condition, (and you will certainly be in a *much worse*, if you see not yourself in this, before you die)—your friends come to comfort you; one brings you an account of a *Saviour*, who was " a mere man"—" the son of *Joseph*

* Pf. xl. 12.

and *Mary*," naturally engendered of the offspring of *Adam*, and, of course, " naturally weak, fallible, " peccable, as yourself, or any " other man," and tells you that he lived about 1787 years ago, was a great teacher of morals, and set a good example: that he " is " not present with us—it is not in " his power to help us—and there- " fore no object of prayer;" and that the idea of *atonement* for sin is " a corruption of the Gospel."

Another comes and tells you of a creature, which he calls a *created God*, a sort of *Deus minorum gentium*. This *being* is " not the pro- " per object of prayer," says he; " he is not continually present
" with

"with us, and a witness to all
"our thoughts and desires *."—
"Then he can have nothing to
"do with the sorrows of my
"wretched heart"—say you.

O but, replies your low *Arian* friend, "he made an atonement "for sin."—What, say you, one *creature* atone for another!—"My "heart recoils at the idea!"— Observe, Sir, I am now supposing you to be awakened to some *real* sense of the *evil* of sin, which you will easily perceive (and this by your own feelings) that your friend, be he high or low *Arian*, is not; and this, because he knows nothing of the obligatory nature of the divine law upon every crea-

* See Letters, p. 113.

ture, be he ever so high, to obey it for himself; and, therefore, that no created being can deserve or merit for others.

Methinks I hear you, in the anguish of *a wounded spirit**, intreating such friends to depart; telling them, as *Job* did his, chap. xiii. 4. *Ye are forgers of lies; ye are all physicians of no value; miserable comforters are ye all!* chap. xvi. 2. —Lest I make this letter too long, I will here break off, leaving what is here said to your serious meditation. My next letter will be my last; after which, you will have no farther trouble from,

SIR,

Yours, &c.

* Prov. xviii. 14.

LETTER XIV.

SIR,

HAVING gotten rid of your *miserable comforters*, you are left in company with a still worse; I mean, your own miserable, disconsolate,* deceitful, and corrupted heart; *every imagination of the thoughts of which* you now are supposed to see (as the Searcher of it sees it) to have been *evil, only evil, and that continually.* Gen. vi. 5. and viii. 21.—With *David,* when he was led to trace the streams of *actual* sin up to their

* See Jer. xvii. 9.

true fountain-head, *natural corruption*, you will confess yourself a *transgressor from the womb*.—Behold! I was shapen in wickedness, and in sin did my mother conceive me†.*—You will *know that the law is spiritual, but that you are carnal; sold under sin.* Rom. vii. 14. This will account for all your opposition to God, in thought, word, and deed; and prove to you, that every book which you have published against the antient Gospel, has been produced by *the ignorance that is in you, through the blindness of your heart* ‡—that the idol of a God *in one person*, which you have

---

* If. xlviii. 8. † Pf. li. 5. ‡ Eph. iv. 18.

set

set up against the *Aleim* of *Israel*, is a creature of the *imagination of the thoughts of your heart*—and that your stepping forth, *Goliah-like*, to defy the armies of the אלהים חיים the LIVING ALEIM, is a sad proof, that you are naturally ignorant, as he was, of the danger of such an attack.

In this view of yourself, Sir, you will have done with ecclesiastical historians, fathers, councils—all vain reasonings, and all traditions of men—you will see, that all your wisdom is folly; your learning, ignorance; your best righteousness, splendid iniquity; that you are guilty, helpless, and hopeless; you will see cause to *abhor your-*
self,

self, and *repent in duſt and aſhes*, in the views of God's holineſs (ſee Job xlii. 5. 6.) and your own ſinfulneſs; and you will cry in the bitterneſs of your heart, as the *Apoſtle* did, when he ſaw all this of himſelf, in the glaſs of the law— *Wretched man that I am! who ſhall deliver me from the body of this death?* Under ſuch convictions, you will no longer ſpeak of the *Devil*, with an "if *there be ſuch an extraordinary being*," or doubt the *Moſaic* account of the fall of *Adam*; for you will perceive, that you have actually been following *Satan*'s example. He deceived our firſt parents*, by contradicting the

* See Gen. iii. 4, 5.

word

word of God, and promising them a superior degree of wisdom by following his suggestions;—the very method which you have taken with your readers, and especially with " the *young men*, who " are in a course of education for " the *Christian ministry*, at the uni- " versities of *Oxford* and *Cambridge*;" whom you would persuade, " that the popular doctrine " of a *soul* has no foundation in " reason, or the Scriptures, but " was borrowed from the heathen " philosophy; and is of no conse- " quence *in itself*, or *to a Christian*, " but as an argument for a future " life." *Letters*, p. 72.—All these things will aggravate your sorrows; and,

and, with the convinced *Paul,* you will subscribe yourself *the chief of sinners;* all your *Babel* of wisdom and vain philosophy will tumble about your ears; all the shrines which you have been making for your great *Diana—Socinianism—*will be destroyed, and you will be glad to hear of one, *who is a Saviour to the uttermost, of all that come to God by him, even Jesus Christ, the same yesterday, to-day, and for ever.* God *over all blessed for ever!*

I now, Sir, take my leave. I have borne my testimony: it has been useful to myself, and I pray God it may be so to others. As to yourself, Sir, remember the awful difference between the Apostle *Paul* and you.—*He preached the faith*

faith which once he destroyed;—you are now destroying the faith which you once preached. Take warning, Sir, ere it be too late.

HE THAT DESPISED MOSES' LAW DIED WITHOUT MERCY, UNDER TWO OR THREE WITNESSES.

OF HOW MUCH SORER PUNISHMENT, SUPPOSE YE, SHALL HE BE THOUGHT WORTHY, WHO HATH TRODDEN UNDER FOOT THE SON OF GOD, AND HATH COUNTED THE BLOOD OF THE COVENANT, WHEREWITH HE WAS SANCTIFIED*, AN UN-

* He was sanctified] i. e. *set apart*, as the antitype of the priests under the law, who were consecrated by putting the blood of the typical sacrifices upon them. See Exod. xxix. 20; by which was prefigured, what is here spoken of.

HOLY THING*, AND HATH DONE DE-SPITE TO THE SPIRIT OF GRACE?

As for any thing which you may say to me, or of me, if you take these letters otherwise than they are meant, and they should offend you, I shall not complain; for you cannot use me worse, than you have used the GOD whom I profess to worship.

I am,

SIR, &c.

---

* An unholy thing.] Κοινος, signifies *common*, that which is in *common use, not sanctified, consecrated,* or *set apart* to any holy use. This is exactly the view which *Socinianism* would teach us to entertain of the *blood of the covenant*; that is, of the BLOOD OF CHRIST, shed, in pursuance of his undertaking in the *covenant* of redemption, for the remission of sins. See Matt. xxvi. 28.

POST-

POSTSCRIPT.

YOU will observe, Sir, that I have not addressed you as a *minister* * of the *Gospel*. In this view,

---

* I would just observe, that though Dr. *P.* is called a *Dissenting minister*, yet he has entirely renounced all benefit from the *Act of Toleration*, 1 Will. and Mary, c. 18; for that truly *Christian* law, which was made for " the ease of scrupulous consciences in the " exercise of religion," expressly exempts from its protection any " person that shall " deny, in his preaching or writing, the doc- " trine of the Blessed Trinity, as it is de- " clared in the 39 Articles, *Sect.* 17." See *Art.* 1.

Dr.

view, a very ſtriking contraſt might have been drawn between you and St.

Dr. *P.* has not only denied the doctrine, as declared in the 39 *Articles*, but declares, "that every poſſible definition of it implies an abſurdity;" nay, "that the *fact* of the *Trinity in Unity* muſt exiſt * in ſome manner or other——that every conceivable mode or manner implies an impoſſibility——and therefore the exiſtence of the thing itſelf muſt be impoſſible alſo." See Letters, p. 27.———In ſhort,

GRÆCUM *eſt non poteſt legi.*

Dr. *P.* is ſometimes for joining *reaſon* and *ſcripture* together, in matters of religious controverſy; but here *ſcripture* is totally put out

---

* This is,
——To tread the high PRIORI road,
And argue downward 'till we doubt of GOD.
POPE.

St. *Paul*; and, to say truth, I cannot recollect a single doctrine in which

of the question, and the Doctor exhibits on the strength of his reason alone. This has produced an argument, which proves (and it proves nothing else) the *pride, folly,* and *ignorance* of the human heart; which can conclude a matter to be *impossible,* because a poor short-sighted mortal cannot conceive the *mode or manner* of *its existence,* or even attempt to *define* it, without involving himself in *absurdity.*

I could wish the Doctor to apply certain questions, which were put, on a very serious occasion, by *Zophar the Naamathite, Job* xi. 7. viz. *Canst thou, by searching* (by all the most minute and curious researches of thine own wisdom) *find out God? Canst thou find out the Almighty to perfection?* i. e. so as fully to comprehend or define his *essence, ways,* or *works?*—Ver. 8. *It is as high as heaven,*

which you agree. No art of reasoning that we are acquainted with,
can

ven, what canst thou do?—deeper than hell, what canst thou know? The measure thereof is longer than the earth, and broader than the sea. ver. 9.

The awful manner in which the above is enlarged upon by the great and incomprehensible JEHOVAH, ch. xxxviii. &c. brought *Job* (who was almost as righteous and wise, *in his own eyes*, as Dr. *P.*) to the very dust. *Behold*, says he, *I am vile; what shall I answer thee? I will lay mine hand upon my mouth. Once have I spoken, but I will not answer; yea, twice, but I will proceed no farther.* ch. xl. 3—5.—And again, ch. xlii. *I have uttered things that I understood not—things too wonderful for me, which I knew not.* ver. 3.—*I have heard of thee by the hearing of the ear; but now mine eye seeth thee*, ver. 5; *wherefore I abhor myself, and repent in dust
and

can possibly reconcile flat contradictions; and therefore, as sensible

and ashes. ver. 6. Go—thou wretched *disputer of this world*—thou *that art darkening counsel by words without knowledge*—thou, that art

" Most ignorant of what thou art most
" assured;"

Go thou, *and do likewise.*

Dr. P.'s notions of *Toleration* are also very curious, as may be seen by his short observations on the *Sermon* of Dr. *Purkis.*— See Lett. p. 68—70. It may be allowed, that one man has no right to *persecute* another, and that *Jews* or *Mahommedans* have as much right to persecute *Christians,* as *Christians* have to *persecute them.*—But, as the *Christian Religion* is part of the *common law* of this country—as (to their *honour* and our *happiness* be it spoken) our *kings* are its NURSING-FATHERS,

ble of this, you endeavour to get rid of so powerful an opponent, by lessening,

FATHERS, and our *queens* its NURSING-MOTHERS — so it has been always held, that *blasphemy* and *profaneness*, written, printed, or advisedly spoken, against it, are indictable and punishable; and who ever heard, that punishments inflicted for *these*, either by *common law*, or by *statute* (See 9 and 10 W. c. 32, which was made in the very *zenith* of civil and religious liberty, against " persons openly avowing and publishing " blasphemous and impious opinions, con- " trary to the doctrines of the Christian Re- " ligion, greatly tending to the dishonour " of Almighty God, and may prove destruc- " tive to the peace and welfare of this king- " dom") were ever deemed *persecution*, any more than convicting a person of *profane cursing* and *swearing*, under 19 G. II. c. 21, and punishing him accordingly?

To

lessening, nay, even by denying his authority; for surely nothing short

To " the TRIUMPH OF TRUTH, or, the " trial of Mr. *Elwall*, for heresy and blas- " phemy, at *Stafford* assizes, before judge " *Denton*," Pr. 2d.—which Dr. *P.* has published among his works—he should have added that of the famous *William Woolston*, for his blasphemous " discourses on the mi- " racles of our Saviour"—and the more modern trial of *Peter Annet*, for a blasphemous libel in the weekly papers, called " The " *Free Inquirer*."

Not but one should think, that " Dr. *P.*'s " works complete, at 15 *l*. 10 *s*. in boards," might furnish matter for a trial at the next *Stafford* assizes, equally edifying and interesting, by way of a *second part* of the TRIUMPH of TRUTH, if the *Grand Jury* of that *county* should be disposed to make the experiment.

The *judge*, no doubt, before whom such an

short of this can be implied, by saying, " that he reasons inconclu-
" sively :"

indictment should be tried, would permit the publication of the *trial*, for the edification of the public, and particularly of that part of it, " who are in a course of education for the
" *Christian* ministry, at the universities of
" *Oxford* and *Cambridge*."

However, Dr. *P.* makes himself perfectly easy on this score. He owns that *he is not protected as a pastor—that he is liable to have all his goods confiscated, and to be imprisoned for life*; which, by the way, is going rather too far; see *Burn*, tit. *Blasphemy* and *Profaneness*.—But " *he has such confidence in the* GOOD
" SENSE *of his countrymen, that he has little*
" *doubt, but that he shall be suffered to go on*
" *as he has hitherto done, unmolested, promot-*
" *ing by every means in his power what he*
" *deems to be important truth, though our le-*
" *gislators in the last century voted it to be*
" HERESY

"sively:" and that "the writings
"of this apostle abound with ana-
"logies and antitheses, on which
"no very serious stress is to be
"laid."

You seem well satisfied, and pleased with your opinions; and say,

"HERESY and BLASPHEMY—alluding, no
"doubt, to the 9 and 10 W. c. 32. above-
"mentioned. However, if I cannot obtain
"a legal *toleration* (says he) *I am very thank-
"ful for a connivance.*"—See Dr. *P.* to Dr.
Horsley, Lett. 17.

The *Italians* have a proverb, which says:

*Tanto va la Capra zoppa,
Che nel Lupo alfin s'intoppa.*

Of which we may, perhaps, one day see an *experimental* illustration, by that profound

say, "Whether we be apt to keep our opinions a longer or a shorter time, they please us so long as we call them *ours*." This was probably the case with

Theologist, that great מפענח צפנות *, that *unfolder of mysteries*—

JOSEPH PRIESTLEY, LL.D. F.R.S.

Ac. Imp. Petrop. R. Paris. Holm. Taurin. Aurel. Med. Paris. Harlem. Cantab. Americ. et Philad. Socius.

Who most nobly, in one of his *mottos* to his letters to Dr. *Horne*, seems to speak with pleasure of the event, in the words of the brave and unfortunate *Achemenides*. Virg. Æn. iii. l. 606.

Si pereo manibus hominum, periisse juvabit.

* See Gen. xli. 45.

those

those teachers among the *Gala-tians*, who were *troubling* and disturbing (ταρασσοντες) *their minds*, by endeavouring to *pervert*, or *subvert*, and *overthrow* (θελοντες μεταςρεψαι) the GOSPEL OF CHRIST. However, these same teachers had very little reason to be pleased with the *new gospel* which they were preaching among their hearers; for the apostle, in plain words, which can have but one meaning, most unreservedly declares—*Though we, or an angel from heaven, preach any other gospel unto you, than that which we have preached unto you,* LET HIM BE ACCURSED. *As we said before, so say I now again, If any preach any other gospel unto you,*

you, than that ye have received, LET HIM BE ACCURSED, Αναθεμα εϛω. You are not to be told, Sir, that the Gr. Αναθεμα, anſwers to the Heb. חרם, which denotes the ſituation of *things,* or *perſons, devoted to deſtruction*; and if this be ſo, may it not be well worth your while to conſider, how far the goſpel which *you* preach, is the goſpel which *Paul* preached, and which the *Galatian* converts had at firſt received? Can you poſſibly have more reaſon to be pleaſed with your *novel* * *opinions,* than *they* had to be pleaſed with *theirs?* more eſpecially, as their departure from the goſpel which the apoſtle

---

* See before, p. 101.

preached, fatal as it might have been, was but *small*, in comparison of what appears in your writings; in all which, not a single lineament of the ancient gospel is to be found, unless to be contradicted or misrepresented.

Under these circumstances, Sir, what can it be to you, whether *Plotinus* was born before *Justin Martyr*, or after him—what *Ebion* held—what *Cerinthus* taught—whether the *Ebionites* or *Nazarenes* existed in the age of the *Apostles*—what were the opinions of the swarms of heretics, which infested the church, during the first and second centuries; of which, by the way, you seem to have adopted
some

some of the very worst? Suppose you can prove your opinions coeval with *heresy* itself, what can any, or all of these, do for you, when you are called to give an account of your ministry? when *the* L*ord cometh with ten thousands of his saints, to execute judgment upon all, and to convince all that are ungodly among them, of all their ungodly deeds which they have ungodly committed, and of all their hard speeches which ungodly sinners have spoken against* H*im*. *Jude* 14, 15.

Nor will all your wisdom, learning, and knowledge, how highly so ever you may rate them, furnish you with a single argument, when you are called upon to shew cause against

against the dreadful *anathema* pronounced by the inspired apostle, if you *finish your course* in your present opinions, which are diametrically opposite to every doctrine of the gospel he preached. *This he certifies* was *not after man, neither was he taught it, but by the revelation of* JESUS CHRIST. *Gal.* i. 11, 12. How very widely *your gospel* differs from this description, you have acquainted your readers, too evidently, to need any farther explanation.

Therefore, leaving these things to your serious consideration, and as to other matters, leaving you, for due correction, to the superior abilities and erudition of Dr. *Horsley*,

Horsley, Mr. *Howes*, and of the amiable and Rev. *Dean* of *Canterbury*, I finally take my leave,

And am, &c. &c.

ADDENDA.

ADDENDA.

DR. P.'s *Arian friend*, in one of his letters to the Doctor, throws two objections in the way of Dr. P.'s scheme of making *Christ* a *mere* man; these are, "that "he is hereafter to *raise all the* "*dead*, and to *judge the world*;"— "Can it be believed (says he) that "a *mere man* could be advanced "*at once* so high, as to be above "angels, and to be qualified to
"rule,

"rule and judge this world?" Here we have one *imaginer* and *reasoner* set against another.

Dr. P. after paying his *friend* a high compliment, on "the piece of "eloquence" in which his argument is delivered, proceeds to answer it:—As to *raising the dead*, "this was done by the old pro"phets before *Christ*, and by the "apostles after him. From this "circumstance, therefore, we are "not obliged to infer that *Christ* "was of a nature superior to that "of man."

Thus the Doctor gets over the first point.

The second—As to *judging the world*, has produced something so
ingenious,

ingenious, so *new*, so *sublime*, as to be *unequalled* by any writer that I ever met with.

Cedite Romani scriptores cedite Graii.

Dr. *Price* argues, that *Christ* is not to be supposed " a *mere man,*
" as it is not *credible*, or even *pos-*
" *sible*, for such an one to be ele-
" vated *at once* into such a degree
" of *knowledge*, as may be requi-
" site to his doing this."

Dr. P. with *two strings* to his bow, thus *shoots his bolt.*—*First*, he answers, " Whatever know-
" ledge may be requisite to his do-
" ing *this* (i. e. *judging the world)*
" may be as easily imparted by
" God,

"God, as the power of raising the
"dead."

Secondly — "When you say,
"that his qualifications for dis-
"charging this office were ac-
"quired *suddenly*, you overlook
"the long interval between his
"ascension and his second com-
"ing, in which you cannot sup-
"pose that he is doing and learn-
"ing nothing." See *Lett*. p. 141
—3.

The old maxim, "LIVE AND
"LEARN," is well-suited to us
short-sighted and ignorant mor-
tals;—but to transfer it, by im-
plication, to the GLORIFIED RE-
DEEMER, is a stretch of *imagination*, a reach of *thought*, a
boldness

boldness of *invention*, a depth of *judgment*, a strength of *reasoning*, which may be supposed to constitute Dr. P. the *admiration* of all his friends, when they see him thus

> "*From vulgar bounds with brave disorder*
> "*part,*
> "*And snatch a grace beyond the reach of*
> "*art.*"
>   POPE Ess. on Crit. l. 154—5.

In short, it out-HERODS *Herod* *, *and his men of war;*
It out-SATANS *Satan* † and his host, or—to say still more,
It out-does Dr. P.'s usual out-doings.

* Comp. Luke xxiii. 11.
† Comp. Mark i. 24.

M   Since

Since writing the above, I have red over the letters of DAVID LEVI to DR. PRIESTLEY.—This honest *Jew* seems much amazed at the Doctor's attempt "to "defend *Christianity* against the "*Jews*;" on such principles as he lays down, and can hardly think, that he is in earnest. "Permit "me, Sir (saith he) to ask you, "whether you sincerely intend, in "this discussion, to defend Chris- "tianity? For your doctrine is "so opposite to what I always un- "derstood to be the *principles of* "*Christianity*, that I must ingenu- "ously confess, I am greatly puz- "zled to reconcile your principles "with the attempt. What! a
"writer

" writer that asserts, that " *the mi-*
" *raculous conception of Jesus does*
" *not appear to him to be sufficiently*
" *authenticated*, and that the *ori-*
" *ginal gospel of St. Matthew did*
" *not contain it*"—" set up for a
" defender of Christianity against
" the Jews! This is such an in-
" consistence, as I little expected
" to meet with in a philosopher,
" whose sole pursuit has been in
" the search of truth." p. 8.

And again, p. 9.—" I must
" however acknowledge, that *you*
" *are pleased* to declare, in plain
" terms, that you " *do not believe*
" *in the miraculous conception of Je-*
" *sus*; and that *you are of opinion,*
" *that he was the legitimate son of*
" *Joseph.*

"*Joseph*. After such assertions as
"these, how you can be entitled
"to the appellation of a Christian,
"in the strict sense of the word,
"is to me really incomprehensi-
"ble."—And p. 30. "If I am
"not greatly mistaken, I verily
"believe, that the honour of Je-
"sus, or the propagation of Chris-
"tianity, are things of little mo-
"ment in your serious thoughts,
"notwithstanding all your boasted
"sincerity."

Dr. P. "professes to write with
"no other view than to make
"proselytes, nor indeed do I see
"(saith he) that there can be any
"other rational object in writing
"at all." *Lett.* p. 93.

I should

I should suppose that Dr. P. is the first who has endeavoured " to " defend *Christianity* against the " *Jews*," by denying what the *Jews* themselves have always understood to be the *principles of Christianity*.

May not DAVID LEVI parody the *apostle*'s words, *Gal.* ii. 14, and say to Dr. P.—" If thou, calling thy-" self a *Christian*, thinkest of " CHRIST after the manner of the " *Jews*, and not as do the *Christians*, why attemptest thou to " defend *Christianity* against the " *Jews?*"

However, this *spirit* of making PROSELYTES to the opinions and doctrines of men, under a notion of converting them to *truth*, being set at work by *human pride*, is very restless; like its FATHER *it goeth about, seeking whom it may devour*—itself may be looked upon as the *parent* of all *sectarian zeal*; we see it operating very strongly in certain *sectaries* of old time, *Matt.* xxiii. 15; through all ages of the *church* ever since; and never will it cease, until the *tares* and the *wheat* shall be finally and everlastingly *discriminated*, by THE GREAT JUDGE OF ALL.

F I N I S.

Other Books Published by Don Milton

Title	Author	Availability
Prince of Sumba Husband to Many Wives	Don Milton	Now
Exhortatory Address to the Brethren in the Faith of Christ	Martin Madan	Now
A Dialog on Polygamy	Bernardino Ochino Don Milton	Now
Thelyphthora Volume I A Treatise on Female Ruin	Martin Madan	May 2009
Thelyphthora Volume II A Treatise on Female Ruin	Martin Madan	May 2009
Thelyphthora Volume III A Treatise on Female Ruin	Martin Madan	May 2009
Juvenal and Persius Volume I	Martin Madan	May 2009
Juvenal and Persius Volume II	Martin Madan	May 2009
John Milton on Polygamy	John Milton	May 2009
Many More Titles	Don Milton & Others	Fall 2009

To Purchase Books or to Contact Don Milton
Visit - DonMilton.com or write:

Don Milton
PO Box 10162
Scottsdale, AZ 85271-0162

www.ingramcontent.com/pod-product-compliance
Lightning Source LLC
Chambersburg PA
CBHW031248290426
44109CB00012B/489